CENTER FOR ISLAM IN THE CONTEMPORARY WORLD
at Shenandoah University

Promoting better understanding of Islam and Muslims in contemporary contexts

www.contemporaryislam.org | Twitter: @CICWatSU

About the Center

The Center for Islam in the Contemporary World (CICW) at Shenandoah University is an academic center engaged in research, teaching, training, and outreach on issues related to Islam and Muslims in contemporary contexts. CICW utilizes interdisciplinary and transdisciplinary approaches from diverse academic specializations. It is involved in education and outreach, connecting Shenandoah University to local, national, and global Muslim communities. CICW is a non-profit, 501(c)(3), tax-exempt private foundation.

Why CICW?

There is an ever-increasing need to understand the global interconnectedness of the world we share. As the second-largest religion in the world, Islam and Muslims occupy an important place in the global landscape of religions, cultures, and societies. CICW contributes to Shenandoah University by connecting Shenandoah University's global orientation to the rich tapestry of contemporary Muslim cultures and societies.

What we do?

- Provide a forum for teaching, learning, and critical engagement with Islam and Muslim societies in contemporary contexts
- Pursue scholarly and intercultural activities that highlight Islam and its relationship with other world religions
- Develop research and training in faith-based and faith-inclusive pedagogies for schools and colleges
- Teach cultural skills, competencies, and literacy necessary for the understanding of Islam and Muslims in contemporary world

Mission

At the Center for Islam in the Contemporary World, we:
- Engage in rigorous and innovative research, education, and outreach to advance a better understanding of Islam and Muslims in diverse, global, and contemporary contexts
- Facilitate collaborations between Shenandoah University and international universities
- Develop training programs for teachers and religious leaders in multi-faith contexts
- Host seminars and lectures on theological and cultural challenges facing Muslims today

Vision

To be known as a globally-recognized center for research and education leading to an enriched understanding of Islamic values and perspectives in a multi-faith world.

The American Masjid

Riad K. Ali

AMERICAN MUSLIMS RESEARCH & DATA CENTER

www.amrdc.com

First Edition

Until recently and apart from few exceptions such as the Islamic Center of Washington, niches and pulpits were not common in the American Masjid. In the few locations that had them, they were not well made or decorated. This is due to the fact that resources were not as good as they are now.

Some of the current designs transcend what you can see in traditional Muslim countries.

Niches & Pulpits

Islamic Community Center of Phoenix

📍 7516 N Black Canyon Hwy | Phoenix, AZ

This is a beautifully designed masjid on both the inside and the outside. It is the largest mosque in Arizona with a 23,000 square foot structure which sits on two acres of land. The structure cost $5.5 million to build. It is topped with a dome that is visible from the nearby highway (I-17). The dome is thirty-six feet in diameter and forty-three feet high, built on top of four half-domes. The niche and pulpit were designed by a Syrian architect from Seattle, and the building was designed by Art and Space Architects and constructed by Kroll Construction. The construction started in 2008 and finished in 2013.

The Islamic Community Center of Phoenix (ICCP) moved into its present mosque (a former church) in 1997. The Center was started by Muslim residents of the north Valley in the early 1980s, and the congregation has moved several times due to the growth of the community.

Scottsdale Mosque

📍 12125 E Via Linda | Scottsdale, AZ

12

The Islamic Center of North East Valley (ICNEV) started planning for the Scottsdale Mosque in August 2013. They received the construction permit a year later and started to build in August 2014. The masjid was inaugurated in Ramadan 2015.

The 4,570 square foot facility is comprised of two floors; a ground floor (3,435 square feet) and an upper floor (1135 square feet). The masjid accommodates 600 people (420 on the ground floor and 180 on the upper floor). It is located on 3.34 acres of land and the total cost of the building was $1.2 million.

The outside structure has one minaret that is forty-five feet high and one dome that is thirty-three feet high and twenty-four feet in diameter. The dome was built from fiberglass in one piece and lifted into place. The beautiful minbar was built in progressive layers, with a traditional patterning screen. The breathtaking mihrab's size was based on the scale of the prayer space and a need for clear sound and viewing.

The project took two years with a cost of $1.25 million from design to opening.

The Institute of Knowledge started in 1998 but construction of the masjid didn't start until May 2012. Soon after that, it was completed. The land size is 16,289 square feet, and the multi-story facility size is a spacious 30,328 square feet that can accommodate 550 people. The whole building project cost $3.8 million to complete.

The outside structure contains one copper sheet metal minaret with a crescent at forty-eight feet tall and one copper sheet metal dome with a crescent that is thirty feet in diameter and forty-two feet, nine inches high. The prayer hall is both elegant and serene with a solid wood minbar and mihrab, designed and manufactured by Rahim Akbar of Rahim's Wood Gallery in Houston, Texas. The whole facility contains a musalla, full-time school, and a full-time seminary.

The Islamic Society of Orange County (ISOC) was established in 1976. Located in Garden Grove, California, in the heart of Orange County, ISOC is within a short commute to major freeways and shopping plazas. Situated among ISOC's 5.2 acres is a full-time accredited K-8 institution, the Orange Crescent School (OCS).

Masjid Al-Rahman

📍 9752 13th St | Garden Grove, CA

Islamic Center of Irvine
📍 2 Truman St | Irvine, CA

The organization was initiated in 2001 and the masjid construction project started in 2002. It took until August 2004 to complete at a total cost of $2 million. The building sits on 1.35 acres of land and the facility is a total of 10,200 square feet (first floor: 7,480 square feet, second floor: 2,720 square feet).

There are no minarets or domes on the outside of the building, but two interior ribbed design ceiling domes exist on the inside at twenty-four feet high and ten feet in diameter. The stunning minbar and mihrab were designed by Architect Shakil Patel and the beautiful Quranic wall murals were painted by Persian artist Mohammad Mujtahidi.

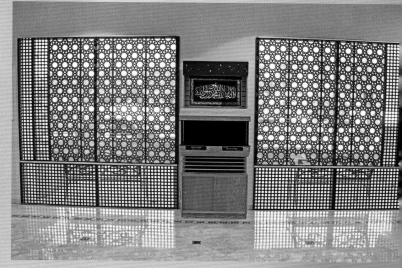

The Orange County Islamic Foundation (OCIF) was established in 1995. One year later, a 24,000 square foot business building was acquired for $1.45 million and converted into a masjid, a school, and a 7,000 square foot rental facility with a nice, metal dome. The remodeling cost $600,000 for the school and $900,000 for the masjid. Beautiful geometric wooden panels cover all windows from the inside and three colorful inner domes with the names of Allah and Mohammad (PBUH) add a magnificent look to the ceiling.

Mission Viejo Masjid
23581 Madero Dr | Mission Viejo, CA

In 1983, the Islamic Center of San Gabriel Valley (Masjid Quba) purchased a derelict Catholic Church on Walnut Drive for $125 thousand. Renovations started immediately to convert the building into a beautiful masjid.

Masjid Quba
📍 19164 E Walnut Dr N | Rowland Heights, CA

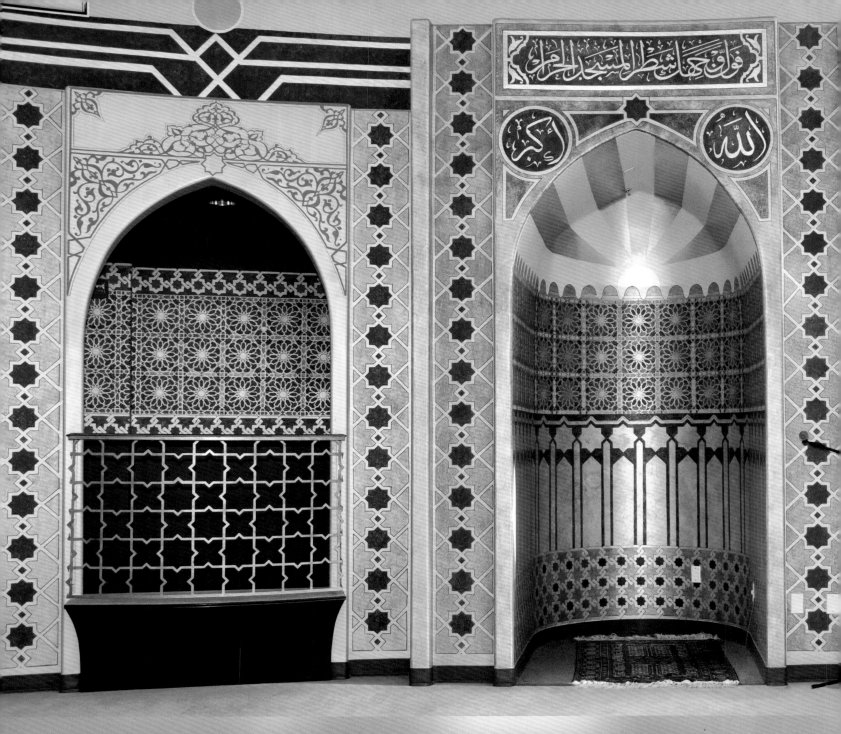

The Sacramento League of Associated Muslims (SALAM) was established on February 24, 1987. On June 18, 1993, SALAM purchased a 2.5-acre property on College Oak Drive with two houses on it. A three-phase plan was designed by Rafat Alafranji. Each phase was implemented according to the availability of funds.

The work on Phase I started in June 1996 and was completed by the end of that summer. The cost of this phase was slightly over $250 thousand. The temporary masjid was opened for Fajr and Isha prayers in October 1997. A month later, the masjid was opened for the first time for Friday prayer on November 7.

Construction of the Phase II building (a 16,000 square foot multi-purpose building for an Islamic school and religious and social meetings) and a parking area started in April 2001 and was completed in February 2002. The architectural plan of

the building was a tasteful combination of East and West. It borrowed the Renaissance window rhythm of arched and square windows on the first and second floor, banded with exterior colored stripes reminiscent of the Middle Eastern Islamic architecture of the Mamluk era. The building was topped with a metal green roof (a popular Islamic color) while projecting contemporary California architectural style. The interior design including the skylight and color scheme was inspired by local buildings. The new structure cost $2.5 million and was dedicated on February 23, 2003.

Construction of the 22,000 square foot SALAM Masjid (Phase III), was started on March 29, 2008 and concluded on August 11, 2010. It cost about $4.5 million. The circular hall opens to a sixty-two foot wide, twenty-seven foot high domed ceiling and accommodates 600 people. The design includes nine verses from Surat Fatir (The Qur'an 35:27-35) on the soffit in a beautiful calligraphy.

The Adhan has NOT been called

SALAM COMMUNITY CENTER

SALAM Islamic Center
📍 4545 College Oak Dr | Sacramento, CA

Bosnian-American Islamic Cultural Center

📍 595 Franklin Ave | Hartford, CT

The migration of Bosniaks to Hartford began in 1997 and ended in 2002.

In the summer of 2007, Hartford Bosnians purchased a space that had previously belonged to a church and was 12,700 square feet. The building was expanded to add five domes and two minarets in 2015.

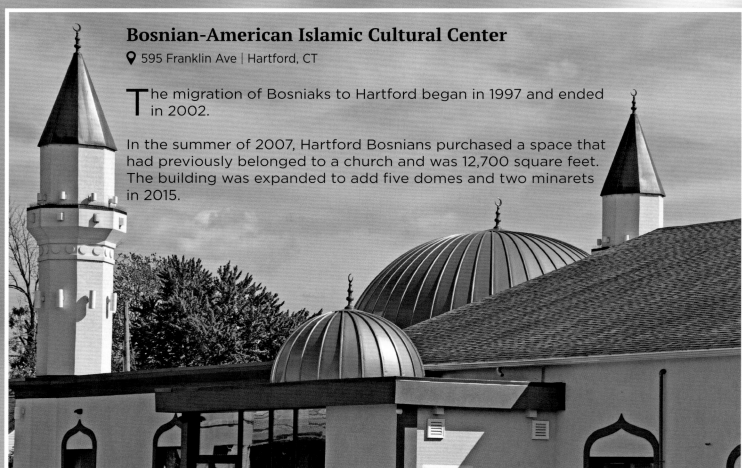

Muhammad's Mosque

📍 1519 4th St NW | Washington, DC

Muhammad's Temple of Islam No. 4 aka Mosque No. 4 was incorporated in 1959. Several adjacent lots were purchased on 4th Street, between P Street SE and Q Street SE, to be the site of a new temple, which would become the second mosque in Washington DC.

In 1960, Malcolm X donated $1.4 thousand and the building was established. It was the first masjid structure to be built from the ground up.

25

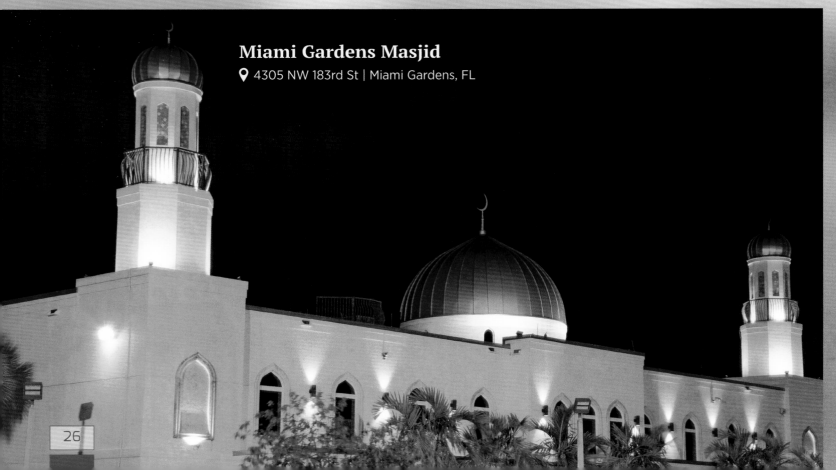

Miami Gardens Masjid

📍 4305 NW 183rd St | Miami Gardens, FL

This organization dates back to 1974. At some point, they purchased five acres of land to construct the current 14,000 square foot facility of the masjid. The $2 million building project started in 1988, and the current facility opened its doors in 2014.

Two side minarets and a center golden dome adorn the outside structure. The inside of the masjid is a peaceful atmosphere for worship with a mihrab from Saudi Arabia and a beautiful carpet from Jordan. The side calligraphy was done by a Turkish calligrapher from Orlando.

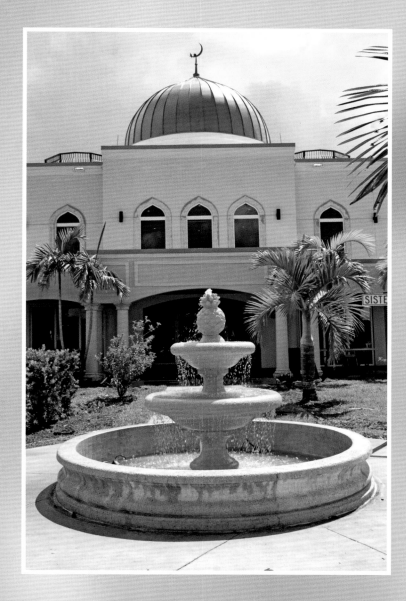

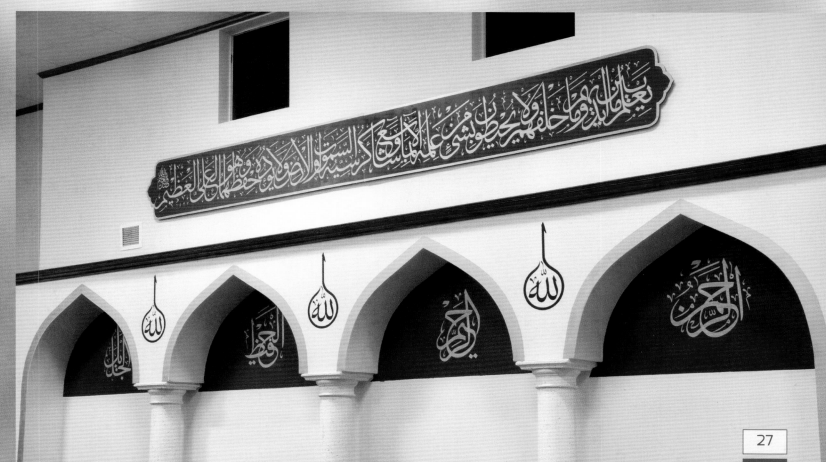

This masjid was established in 1980 as The Atlanta Mosque, a nonprofit, non-political, religious organization. Later due to a name conflict with another organization, its name was changed to Al-Farooq Masjid of Atlanta.

In 1982, the Masjid Board acquired five acres of land to establish a Muslim cemetery. This facility, with a burial capacity of 2,000, is one of the very few Muslim cemeteries available in this country. To date, approximately 300 Muslims from various parts of the country have been buried in this cemetery.

In 1990, the masjid decided to expand the scope of its service activities by establishing an academic religious-parochial school (Dar-un-Noor School), teaching grades pre-K through 8. The Atlanta Dar-ul-Uloom was added in 1994 as a boarding Quran and Hifz school.

Al-Farooq Masjid of Atlanta

📍 442 14th St NW | Atlanta, GA

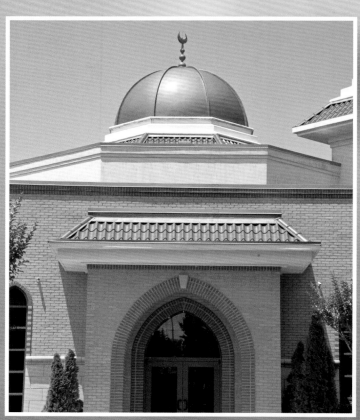

Dalton Islamic Center
📍 2054 Dug Gap Rd | Dalton, GA

Albanian American Islamic Center
5825 Saint Charles Rd | Berkeley, IL

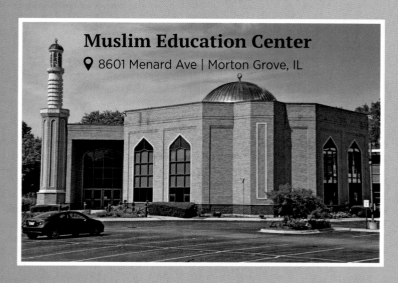

Muslim Education Center
📍 8601 Menard Ave | Morton Grove, IL

Muslim Education & Cultural Center of America

📍 16W560 91st St | Willowbrook, IL

Muslims began settling in Lexington, Kentucky in the early 1970s and a small group became organized in 1975.

In 1978, after renting and being displaced from several facilities, a permanent location at 572 Georgetown Street became the first masjid in Lexington.

After renting at the location for over two decades, Masjid Bilal took ownership of the Georgetown Street property in 2001. The community purchased a 2.4-acre property at 1545 Russell Cave Road in March 2004 which became the current location of the masjid.

In January 2014, after years of fundraising, the community began the construction of a new masjid at the Russell Cave location in front of the existing masjid. It was completed in the fall of 2015 and the community took occupancy in October that year.

Masjid Bilal Ibn Rabah

📍 1545 Russell Cave Rd | Lexington, KY

Islamic House of Wisdom

📍 22575 Ann Arbor Trl | Dearborn Heights, MI

Masjid Al-Salam

📍 4630 S Irvington Ave | Tulsa, OK

Respect Graduate School
 2200 Industrial Dr | Bethlehem, PA

The RGS Masjid is a breathtaking prayer room. Visitors are mesmerized by its three domes and mihrab. Each dome is hand-painted with Islamic calligraphy, the entrance doors are carved with a beautiful assortment of geometric shapes and the walls are adorned with the gilded panels and blue ceramic tiles that are typically found in mosques around the world.

Muslim American Society of Philadelphia
123 E Luzerne St | Philadelphia, PA

Masjid Al-Rahman

📍 1901 Kelly Blvd | Carrollton, TX

In the deep south of Texas and very close to the border of Mexico, this 10,000 square foot mosque was constructed in 2005 on 2.5 acres for a cost of $2 million and a capacity of 700 worshippers.

Two minarets that are sixty-five feet tall from the ground up and three domes (twenty feet high and twenty-four feet in diameter) mark the Islamic appearance of the building from outside. The gorgeous niche and pulpit was imported from Syria along with the chandelier.

Masjid Arridwan
📍 1910 Elsham Rd | Edinburg, TX

Masjid Arridwan

📍 1910 Elsham Rd | Edinburg, TX

MAS Katy Center
📍 1800 Baker Rd | Houston, TX

Future home of the MAS Katy Center

Katy is a suburb of Houston, Texas located twenty-five miles west of downtown. It is a primarily middle to upper class area with a large Muslim community. In 2006, an eleven acre plot of land was purchased in an affluent residential area with hopes of it becoming the home of the first complete Islamic center in Katy. Late in 2007, a master plan was put together for the entire plot of land. Phase One, with a budget of $1.1 million started in July 2009 after securing all the required construction permits. The new prayer hall was completed in April 2010. The parking lot expansion project was completed in April 2011, and the community welcomed the start of the new masjid construction in 2012.

The center houses a full-time Islamic school, a Quranic academy, and Al-Huda University.

In 2016, MAS Katy took another step towards building an exemplary community by purchasing an adjacent ten acres, this made the MAS Katy land a twenty-one acre facility, one of the biggest Islamic centers in the south.

Islamic Center of San Antonio

📍 8638 Fairhaven St | San Antonio, TX

The Islamic Center of San Antonio was established in 1993. They purchased a ten-acre piece of land to construct the masjid on. The project started in 1996 and the new masjid was opened by Ramadan of 2012.

The facility is a spacious 21,500 square feet in size and has a capacity of around 2000 people. The final cost of the building was $3 million, which was generously donated by the community. The outside structure has two minarets that are thirty feet tall each and one gold trimmed dome (twenty feet high and seventeen feet in diameter). The masjid's old building was converted into a full-time Islamic school.

On the inside there is a breathtaking all marble mihrab in a washed stone design with a three-foot-high marble podium, and a ten foot projection screen for presentations. The facility has a Da'wah room, a babysitting room, two split women sections, a youth activity room, wide hallways, and a hidden shoe area. There is Islamic art on the ceiling and Islamic art medallions throughout.

Architect Kimly Mangum designed Masjid Khadeeja in 1992 on 2.75 acres of land. Its gold dome and towering minaret are visible from the freeway and the westbound TRAX line. Khadeeja's first structure was completed in 1994 at about 5,000 square feet. Expansions followed, and the center was fully completed in 2002 growing to a size of 15,000 square feet after they acquired several acres east and west of the center. Future plans are being made to add an Islamic school and a community hall.

Khadeeja Masjid
📍 1019 W Parkway Ave | West Valley City, UT

ADAMS Center
46903 Sugarland Rd | Sterling, VA

Islamic Center of Southern California | Los Angeles, CA

Albanian American Culture & Islamic Center
Waterbury, CT

Islamic Foundation | Villa Park, IL

Islamic Community Ctr of Illinois | Chicago, IL

Stamford Islamic Center | Stamford, CT

Islamic Society of Akron and Kent
Cuyahoga Falls, OH

Masjid Al-Islam | Bolingbrook, IL

Shahid Mosque | Charlotte, NC

Hoover Crescent Islamic Center | Hoover, AL

Dar Alarkam Mosque | Red Oak, TX

Masjid Un Noor | Staten Island, NY

Masjid Al-Noor | South Bend, IN

Masjid Al-Israa | Fridley, MN

Masjid Al Kauthar | Wilmington, DE

Masjid Ar-Rahman | Memphis, TN

Masjid Al-Rahman | Orlando, FL

Islamic Ctr of Golden | Golden, CO

Chino Valley Islamic Center | Chino, CA

Masjid Hazrat Abu Bakr Siddiq | St. Louis, MO

Masjid e Tauhid | San Diego, CA

ICCNY Riverside | New York, NY

Masjid Al-Salaam | Dearborn, MI

Masjid Al Noor | Westminster, CA

Islamic Center of South Florida
Pompano Beach, FL

Denver International Airport Mosque | Denver, CO

Muslim Community of Western Suburbs | Canton, MI

Bosnian Islamic Center | St. Louis, MO

Masjid Omar Ibn Al-Khatab | Tuscaloosa, AL

Masjid Ibraheem | Newark, DE

Parkchester Jame Masjid | Bronx, NY

Islamic Center of Kansas | Olathe, KS

Islamic Center of Modesto | Modesto, CA

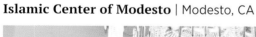

Clifton Blue Mosque | Clifton, NJ

Islamic Center of Little Rock
Little Rock, AR

Islamic Education Ctr of OC
Costa Mesa, CA

Masjid Al Salaam | Dunedin, FL

Cactus Islamic Center | Cactus, TX

Islamic Society of Germantown
Germantown, MD

Islamic Foundation North
Libertyville, IL

Jerrahi Order of America | Spring Valley, NY

Muslim Center of New York | Flushing, NY

Masjid An-Noor | Bridgeport, CT

Islamic Center of Harrison
Harrison, NJ

Masjid Assunnah
Stone Mountain, GA

Masjid Aysha | Lakeland, FL

Masjid Granada Hills | Granada Hills, CA

Islamic Center of Detroit | Detroit, MI

For the most part of the 20th century, mosques were converted from other places of worship, homes, commercial facilities, or other pre-established buildings which meant they often did not have a dome nor a minaret. In a few instances, communities added a minaret to the existing structure to better identify it as a place of worship.

Later, when mosques were constructed from the ground up, domes and minarets became part of the design. Wherever there is a homogeneous community such as Bosnian, Albanian, or Turkish, visitors will notice a great resemblance of the structure to those from the group's homeland. On the other hand, when the community is heterogeneous, the minaret often takes on its own unique look.

Domes & Minarets

Islamic Center of East Valley

📍 425 N Alma School Rd | Chandler, AZ

The ICEV started in 1997. Later, they purchased five acres of land and the construction of the masjid started in 2004. The masjid opened its doors in the third quarter of 2008 with a facility of 13,000 square feet that held 750 people. The cost of the project was $4.4 million.

The facility has one dome that is thirty feet high and sixteen feet in diameter, two stories and a basement. The first floor is a men's prayer hall and lobby, and the second floor is the women's exclusive prayer hall. There is an elevator from first to the second floor.

Masjid E Ibrahim

📍 2075 Airway Ave | Kingman, AZ

This location is a 4,000 square foot facility built on 1.5 acres of land that was completed in 1992. It serves a small community of Muslims.

Islamic Center of North Phoenix

📍 13246 N 23rd Ave | Phoenix, AZ

The Islamic Community of Bosniaks in Phoenix was established in 1995 and inaugurated in October 1997 with the presence of Reis-ul-ulema, Mustafa Ceric, Chief Imam Senad Agic and Imam Sabahudin Ceman.

In April 2007, the group purchased a church and remodeled completely in two and a half months. The new center was officially opened in August 2007.

Masjid Jauharatul-Islam
📍 102 W South Mountain Ave | Phoenix, AZ

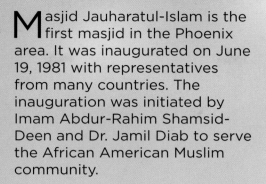

Masjid Jauharatul-Islam is the first masjid in the Phoenix area. It was inaugurated on June 19, 1981 with representatives from many countries. The inauguration was initiated by Imam Abdur-Rahim Shamsid-Deen and Dr. Jamil Diab to serve the African American Muslim community.

"As awesome as this masjid is at sunset, its beauty is just as magnificent at midday. The whiteness of the stucco building rising on eight acres of desert land brings it into prominence against the beige, brown and peach desert landscape. The three silver balls on the stem of the minaret glisten like diamond jewels in the sun against the backdrop of [the] Rocky Mountains and cerulean blue skies. The walkway leading to the inside and [the] courtyard is flanked by lines of [o]range, [g]rapefruit and [l]emon trees that scent the air and brush the senses with the sweet smell of honey and blossoms. The wide, wooden front door is outlined in 3-D with blue and white marble tile inscribed with 'Allah-u-Akbar' in Arabic calligraphy.

Upon entering, one steps into a cool courtyard strategically built to not only be cooler than the surrounding desert but to also capture any breeze. In the middle of the square courtyard lies [velvety-thick,] green grass surrounded by various flowering plants and an orange clay water fountain from Mexico gurgling cool water in the center.

As one walks along the blue, [marble-tiled] walkway, there are stucco arches outlined with blue and white hand swirled tiles donated [by] families from Turkey and strong oak doors leading to the entrance of the masjid prayer area. On the opposite side, the walkway leads to another area of thoughtful

introspection called the ˜jannah" (heaven). Here there is a blue clay water fountain, as well as [o]range, [l]emon and [l]ime trees [with] plush, overgrown rose bushes that have pink, red, white, yellow or orange petals forming the flowers and flecks of light caught by the three balls of the minaret above glistening off the stucco walls. The mixture of scents from the rose bushes and citrus plants along with tiny white blossoms from the trees that are often floating through the area enhance the spiritual senses. Beyond the walls of this area rises the backdrop of South Mountain to create a picture-perfect scene.

Inside the masjid prayer (mussalah) area are large stucco columns and green shag carpeting almost as thick as the grass in the courtyard. On top of this carpeting are woven rugs from Iran and Afghanistan in rich colors of brown, beige, and maroon with geometric designs. A [carved-out] mihrab is along the front center wall with a window of gold and black [with the words] "Allah-u-Akbar" installed along the top. Six elaborate chandeliers donated [by] the Tung family of China sparkle from the ceiling and pick up the flecks of stone in the stucco walls and the words in the Mihrab." *

*Shamsid-Deen, Mahasin. "Historical Mosque in Phoenix, Arizona Commemorates 25 Years." Article in Latino American Dawah Organization (LADO) Newsletter, October-December 2006

Islamic Community Center of Tempe

📍 131 E 6th St | Tempe, AZ

Tempe Masjid was established in 1984. Its beautiful architecture is modeled after the Dome of the Rock in Jerusalem; the eight-sided structure has a minaret and a gold dome.

The sixty-five foot minaret is an exact replica of the original one. In 2009, it was noticed that the minaret is slanted. Further inspection revealed corrosion on some of the big screws bolting the minaret to the ground which was believed to be attributed to pigeon droppings. For public safety, it was decided to take it down and the minaret was rebuilt in 2011.

Islamic Center of Jonesboro

📍 118 N Rogers St | Jonesboro, AR

The Islamic Center of Jonesboro is one of fifteen Islamic centers in the state of Arkansas and the only masjid in Jonesboro. The masjid was inaugurated on August 17, 1983. The shahada adorns all the outside walls of the masjid. The shahada translates to "There is no God but him and Muhammad is his messenger." This community is mainly made up of students who come to study at Arkansas State University (ASU).

Domes & Minarets

Islamic Center of Pine Bluff

📍 3707 W Hepburn St | Pine Bluff, AR

The Islamic Institute of Orange County started in 1991. The construction of the nearly $4 million structure started in 2001 and was completed in 2005. A marvelous assortment of colorful and carefully assembled decoration tiles imported from Morocco adorn the sixty-eight foot minaret as well as the main entrance. The gorgeous minaret and the golden dome makes it a landmark structure in the area. The 34,000 square foot structure sitting on a 1.25-acre lot is the home of Masjid Omar and Minaret Academy.

Al Masjid Al Jamea

📍 33330 Peace Terrace | Fremont, CA

Masjid Fresno

In 1984, the Islamic Center of Central California was founded and soon after that building of the Masjid of Fresno started. The structure was finally completed in February 1989. The masjid was designed to resemble one in Jedda, Saudi Arabia. The total facility size is 10,000 square feet on 1.25 acres of land. The cost of the building was a modest $400 thousand, very low compared to modern buildings.

There is an interesting story behind the construction of this masjid. The work was managed by Amin Attia who hired subcontractors to do the job. Everything was going well until they came to the construction of the dome. He could not find a contractor to complete the job. Then, an eighty-year-old man stopped by to chat with them and offered directions on a way to do it. They hired an experienced carpenter who prepared a small portal on the ground first. He then constructed and prepared the actual dome and then Attia hired another company from San Francisco to pour eight inches of concrete all around it from the roof to the top of the dome.

The outside structure is simple with a seventy-five foot tall minaret and an approximately fifty foot high dome that's forty-one feet in diameter and is topped with a crescent from Makkah, Saudi Arabia.

Masjid Fresno

📍 2111 E Shaw Ave | Fresno, CA

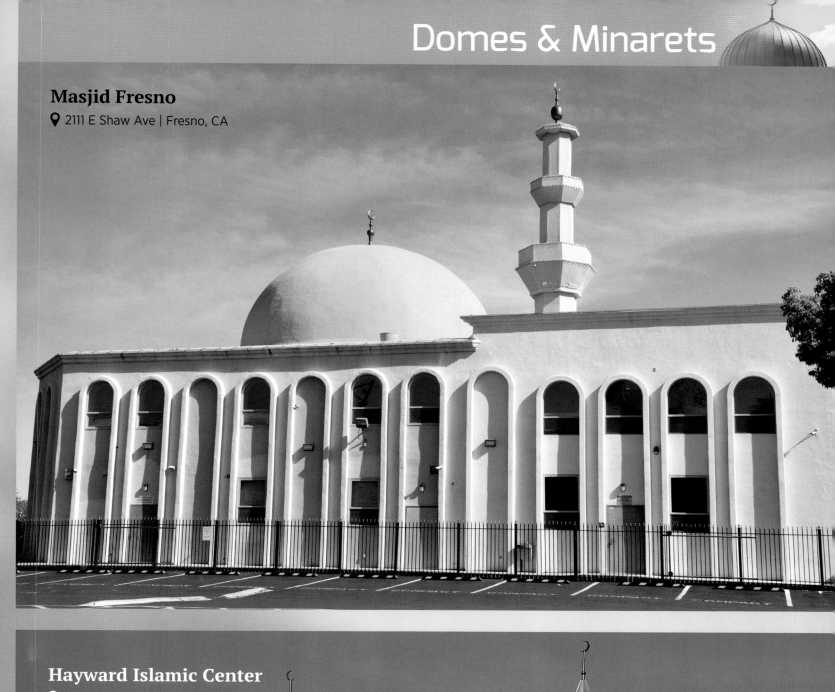

Hayward Islamic Center

📍 26320 Gading Rd | Hayward, CA

Masjid Omar Ibn Al-Khattab

📍 1025 Exposition Blvd | Los Angeles, CA

On January 21, 1994, in time for Ramadan 1414 Hijri, Masjid Omar formally opened its doors. This was the culmination of over fifteen years of work by hundreds of volunteers to establish the first place of worship in Los Angeles that was designed and built as a masjid.

The land for Masjid Omar was bequeathed in 1977 by a mother who fell ill and passed away while visiting her children who were studying at the University of Southern California. Her donation was followed in turn by donations from untold numbers of benefactors to build the masjid on the land.

Masjid Omar is located close to USC and the museums at Exposition Park. It's considered a landmark with a decorated minaret top that soars eighty-three feet in the skies. It also has a very large, dark-green, fiberglass minaret, one of the largest in the US with a fifty foot diameter and a height of thirty feet.

Domes & Minarets

Oakland Islamic Center

📍 515 31st St | Oakland, CA

After humble beginnings as the Muslim Education Community Center of America (MECCA) in 1992, and years of holding activities in a small warehouse on 9th Street, the ICIE purchased land in 1998.

The ICIE encloses over 2.98 acres of land and has been operating as a full-time masjid on these premises since September 2000.

Islamic Center of Inland Empire

📍 9212 Base Line Rd | Rancho Cucamonga, CA

ANY CAR PARKED IN UNAUTHORIZED PARKING SPACE WILL BE TOWED AT OWNERS EXPENSE NOT "ICIE"

9212

O riginally founded in 1989, the Islamic Association of Greater Hartford is one of the first Islamic centers in the state of Connecticut.

Masjid Al-Mustafa

📍 95 Schraffts Dr | Waterbury, CT

After ten years of construction, Masjid Al-Mustafa officially opened its doors on May 19, 2017. The new building, which overlooks I-84 and is the largest mosque in Connecticut, has three floors: the main level contains a large prayer space for men and women as well as a gymnasium, the second floor has several classrooms for Sunday School courses and other educational purposes, and the basement level is a community center and can accommodate events such as dinners and fundraisers.

The total land size of the facility is 3.1 acres and the masjid (3,100 square feet) has a capacity of 1000 people. The total cost of the building was $5 million. It has two steel and fiber glass minarets that are sixty feet high. It also has one fiber glass dome that is ten feet in diameter and fifteen feet high.

Assalam Center of Boca Raton

📍 1499 NW 4th Ave | Boca Raton, FL

Islamic Center of Boca Raton
Q 3480 NW 5th Ave | Boca Raton, FL

The Islamic Center of Boca Raton (ICBR) owns a 3.3-acre lot committed for the masjid/center construction and an adjacent 3.3-acre site with an 11,000 square foot school building.

Construction of the center began in 1999 and the doors were opened in August 2012. The total space of the center is 17,450 square feet and the prayer hall can accommodate 500 people. The total cost of the building came to $3.6 million.

The outside structure has a sixty-five foot, eight inch tall minaret that is constructed from steel and covered with aluminum plates and stucco. It also adorns two domes that are forty-six feet, forty inches tall and twenty-two feet, twelve inches in diameter. Both are also constructed from steel and covered with aluminum plates.

Al Amin Center of Florida

📍 8101 S Military Trail | Boynton Beach, FL

In 1995, the Al Amin Center of Florida was established. One year later, three acres of land in Del Rey beach was purchased for $142 thousand. Payments on the land completed in 1998. Ten additional acres in Del Rey beach were purchased in 1999 and 2000, and five trailers were purchased to serve the weekend school at the first site on Del Rey beach.

Between 2010-2011, additional land (2.8 acres, $610 thousand) was purchased to build the mosque from the ground up in Boynton Beach, Florida. Construction for phase one (ten thousand square feet, $1.9 million) began in September 2012 and concluded in 2014 for a total of $3 million.

Islamic Community of Bosniaks in Jacksonville

📍 2131 Art Museum Dr | Jacksonville, FL

Masjid Al-Jami'

📍 7326 Sligh Ave E | Tampa, FL

Daaru Salaam Mosque

📍 15830 Morris Bridge Rd | Thonotosassa, FL

The idea for the Daaru Salaam Mosque was born when community members purchased a property featuring an existing 2,000 square foot building that was used as a mosque for several years.

Today, a 7,500 square foot, $1.6 million mosque stands on that same property, serving as the primary place of worship for the two to three thousand Muslims of the New Tampa and Wesley Chapel communities.

Masjid of Alpharetta

📍 1265 Rucker Rd | Alpharetta, GA

Masjid of Alpharetta

📍 1265 Rucker Rd | Alpharetta, GA

The Mosque Foundation

📍 7360 W 93rd St | Bridgeview, IL

In 1954, a handful of Palestinian immigrants on Chicago's famous Southside established the Mosque Foundation of Chicago.

Built in 1981 on a few acres of swampy land in the middle of mostly abandoned prairie in Bridgeview, the Mosque Foundation began as a small structure with a maximum prayer hall capacity of 300 worshippers.

As the population of the Muslim community there grew, the need to purchase more property was realized. In 1963, a church located at 6500 S. Steward Ave was purchased and converted into a prayer hall and school for the community of more than a hundred Arab-Muslim families living in the southwest side of Chicago at the time. Several

years later, the building was sold to purchase a storefront property at 79th and Clyde Avenue.

The Clyde property was sold shortly thereafter, with the proceeds reserved to purchase land in Bridgeview, where the mosque currently stands.

Construction began in November 1978, and three years later the doors were officially open.

In 1998, the Foundation expanded its original facility to accommodate the community's growth. In 2002, they purchased a lot for additional parking space, and in 2008, the second major expansion was completed.

Masjid Al-Faatir

◈ 1200 E 47th St | Chicago, IL

In 1983, the doors to a portion of the building of The Muhammad Mosque opened.

The funding for the center was provided by heavy weight champion Muhammad Ali and his manager Jabir Herbert Muhammad. Mr. Jabir's son, Imam Omar is still serving the Masjid to this day.

The summer of 1996 began with the call to prayer being heard from the only minarets in the city of Chicago at Masjid Al-Faatir.

Islamic Comm. Center of Des Plaines

📍 480 Potter Rd | Des Plaines, IL

South Suburban Islamic Center

15200 Broadway Ave | Harvey, IL

Masjid DarusSalam

📍 21W525 North Ave | Lombard, IL

In December 2007, the DarusSalam Foundation purchased a 6.5-acre parcel of land with plans to build a masjid and academy.

The construction of the masjid was completed in July 2013 and its doors opened just days before the start of Ramadan.

In 2015, an additional 3.5-acre parcel of land was purchased and the 22,000-square-foot building now also offers classrooms, resource libraries, a basketball court, a kitchen, and ample parking.

In 2018, Masjid DarusSalam will begin its Phase Two expansion, which will add a dedicated women's prayer hall, academy building, and a gymnasium, among other things.

Domes & Minarets

Islamic Cultural Center of Greater Chicago

📍 1810 N Pfingsten Rd | Northbrook, IL

On September 8, 1974, a groundbreaking ceremony took place in a lot of a little over two acres purchased by BACA (The Bosnian American Cultural Association).

In March 21, 1976, the first phase of the Islamic Cultural Center consisting of administration offices, library, weekend school classes, a nursery, and a social hall opened its doors in a ceremony of the Center's second phase (the mosque and the minaret). The groundbreaking for this phase was held on June 29, 1984. It wasn't long before the first minaret in the area was finished and the mosque's external works were completed.

The Prayer Center of Orland Park

📍 16530 S 104th Ave | Orland Park, IL

On June 21, 2004, the founders of the Prayer Center of Orland Park received the final approval from the Village of Orland Park to move forward with the project of building a masjid. The groundbreaking ceremony took place in October 2004, and construction of the Prayer Center of Orland Park began in earnest.

Throughout the following eighteen months, the founders were responsible for raising the completion funds through the generous contributions of many in the community. Finally, in June 2006, the doors of the Prayer Center of Orland Park opened to the public.

The facility is 22,700 square feet and accommodates 1500 people. The total land size is 10.1 acres and the building project cost $5 million. The fifty-three foot high dome with a diameter of thirty-two feet sits on top of the building that was originally built with fiberglass but was renovated in 2012 with a steel standing-seam roofing.

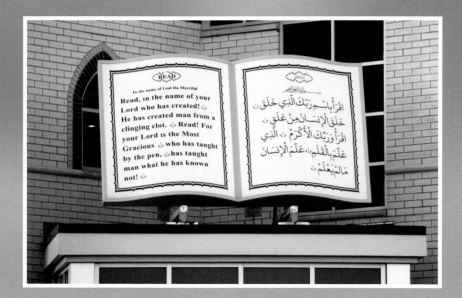

Islamic Center of Peoria

4125 W Charter Oak Rd | Peoria, IL

Muslim Community Center of Greater Rockford

📍 5921 Darlene Dr | Rockford, IL

Masjid Al-Huda

📍 1081 W Irving Park Rd | Schaumburg, IL

Islamic Center of Bloomington
📍 1925 E Atwater Ave | Bloomington, IN

Northwest Indiana Islamic Center
📍 9803 Colorado St | Crown Point, IN

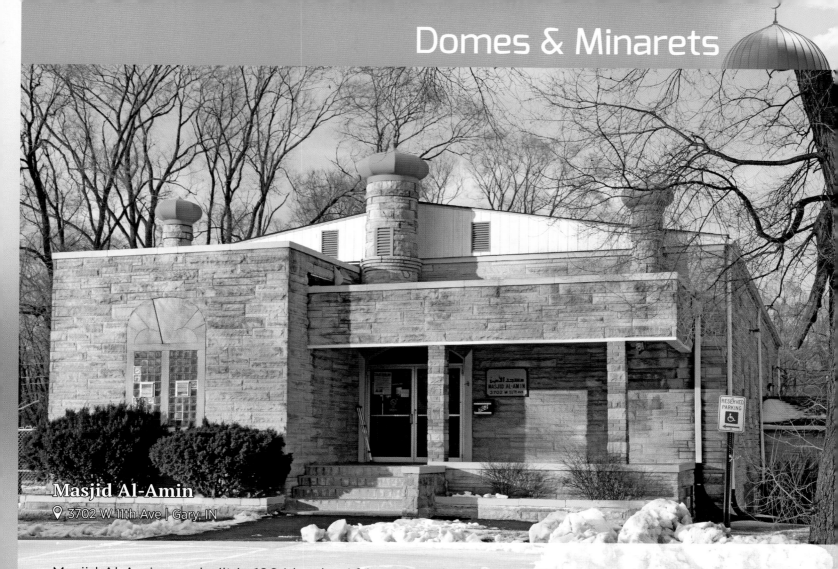

Masjid Al-Amin
◉ 3702 W 11th Ave | Gary, IN

Masjid Al-Amin was built in 1964 by the African-American community as a Sunni masjid. For several years in the 1960s, it served as the headquarter for the Muslim Student Association.

Northwest Indiana Islamic Center

The space that houses the Northwest Indiana Islamic Center was once a vast expanse of corn fields. In 1991, ten acres were bought for $36 thousand.

Construction of this mosque started in October 1992, and the first Friday prayer, attended by nine individuals, occurred about six months later. By 1999, the existing structure had become too small for the needs of the community and a new prayer hall and a multipurpose gymnasium and community center was built. This was followed by the establishment of a full-time school, a Sunday school, and a three day-per-week school.

Masjid Al-Fajr

📍 2846 Cold Spring Rd | Indianapolis, IN

Islamic Center of Michigan City

📍 1606 N 500 E | Michigan City, IN

The Islamic Society of North America (ISNA) traces its origins to a meeting of several Muslim student organizations in January 1963, at which the Muslim Students Association of the US and Canada (MSA) was formed. ISNA regards the MSA's 1963 convention as its first one, held at the University of Illinois at Urbana-Champaign.

The present-day ISNA was founded in 1982 through a joint effort of four organizations: The Muslim Students Association of the US and Canada (MSA), the Islamic Medical Association (IMA), the Association of Muslim Social Scientists (AMSS), and the Association of Muslim Scientists and Engineers (AMSE). Many of the leaders of these four founding organizations took leadership roles in the newly formed ISNA. In 1983, ISNA completed a $21 million ($51,598,396 today) headquarters complex in suburban Indianapolis using funds raised in part from international sources.

Source: en.wikipedia.org

Islamic Society of North America

6555 S. County Rd. 750 E | Plainfield, IN

The Mother Mosque of America in Cedar Rapids, Iowa, built in 1934, was once known as The Rose of Fraternity Lodge and also the Moslem Temple. It is the longest standing mosque in North America. The mosque was built by a local community of immigrants and their descendants from areas that are now known as Lebanon and Syria. Construction was completed in February 15, 1934. The small structure served as a place of worship for Muslims for nearly forty years. When a larger local mosque, the "Islamic Center of Cedar Rapids" was built in 1971, the building was sold. Successive owners over the next twenty years allowed it to fall into disrepair. In 1991, the Islamic Council of Iowa purchased the building, refurbished it, and restored its status as a Muslim cultural center.

Masjed El Rahmah

📍 2140 Morgantown Rd | Bowling Green, KY

The first Islamic center in Bowling Green was founded by the local Bosnian community in 1998 on Old Morgantown Road. As the Muslim population of the area continued to grow, the Islamic Center of Bowling Green (ICBG) was opened in May 2005. It is one of three mosques in Bowling Green.

The center includes Masjed el Rahmah, a weekend Islamic school, and an Islamic library in the masjid.

Islamic Center of Elizabethtown

📍 2710 Ring Rd | Elizabethtown, KY

The Islamic Center of Elizabethtown was established in 1985 and has subsequently gone through two expansions in addition to updated facilities. Their current building on Ring Road was completed in 2008 by the architectural firm McCoy Architects LLC. It is a two-story, 13,810 square foot building with a steel frame clad in a concrete brick veneer. A large dome sits atop the prayer hall. The multi-purpose center includes a mosque, meeting rooms, function rooms, and offices. The old facility was located on 2816 Ring Road.

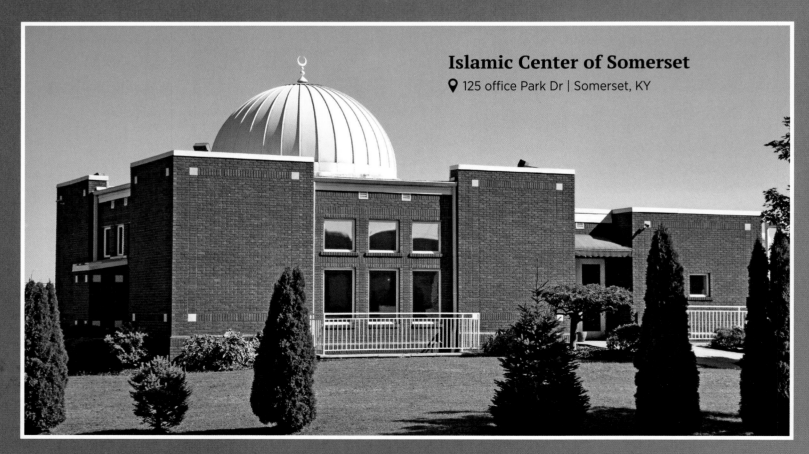

Islamic Center of Somerset

📍 125 office Park Dr | Somerset, KY

The Islamic Center of Somerset opened in 2001, giving a permanent facility to community Muslims who had previous gathered in each other's homes to pray. The Center was designed by McCoy Architects LLC of Lexington, Kentucky. It is a 4,284 square feet, two-story brick building, with a white dome over the prayer hall. Inside, there is a large prayer hall, classrooms, restrooms, a multi-purpose hall, and a kitchen.

Masjid Omar

📍 1528 Pietro Ct | Harvey, LA

Masjid Abu-Bakr Al-Siddiq

📍 4425 David Dr | Metairie, LA

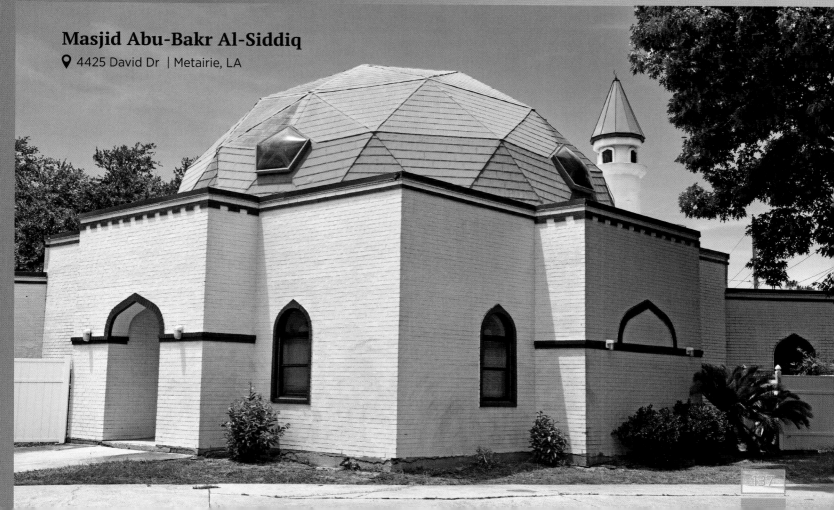

Masjid Al-Rahmah

📍 6631 Johnnycake Rd | Baltimore, MD

The Islamic Society of Baltimore (ISB) was established in 1969.

In 1982, more than a decade later, ISB purchased an eight acre lot at its current location and built Masjid Al-Rahmah. Three years later, a housing complex was built adjacent to the masjid and by 1987, and a full-time primary school had been established.

Within the next ten years, ISB founded the Quran Academy and Sunday school which were in full swing just in time for the completion of the multi-purpose hall in 1997.

The Islamic Society of Germantown is a non-profit, independent organization that was created after years of dedication from a group of fellow Muslims who started working on the idea in 1998.

The groundbreaking of the ISG Masjid occurred on November 8, 2014. There are no other Islamic centers or mosques within a ten mile radius.

Islamic Society of Germantown

9 19825 Blunt Rd | Germantown, MD

Southern Maryland Islamic Center

📍 1046 Solomons Island Rd | Prince Frederick, MD

Six acres of land were donated to the Muslims at the Southern Maryland Islamic Center by Issam Damalouji, one of the first Muslim residents in Calvert County, and a Christian resident. The lot is directly across the street from the hospital, and a 7,448 square foot mosque was constructed on the site. It was completed in 1986 and opened in 1987.

The central portion of the mosque is shaped like an octagon, with another half-octagon shape joined on the eastern side of the building. A large green dome sits above the central section of the mosque, with small clerestory windows around the drum. There is a square minaret, topped by a small green dome, at the northeast corner of the building. Three pointed arches frame the entrance to the building on the eastern side. It is faced with white brick and stucco.

Islamic Society of the Washington Area

📍 2701 Briggs Chaney Rd | Silver Spring, MD

The Muslim Community Center was registered in 1976. The construction for the 6,000 square foot facility sitting on a ten-acre parcel started in 1992 and was completed in 1994. The Masjid is identified easily by its copper dome with a tall minaret on the side. The dome is decorated from the inside with verses from the Quran. The mihrab is made up of simple but elegant cascading rectangles that leave room for future decorations.

Muslim Community Center

📍 15200 New Hampshire Ave | Silver Spring, MD

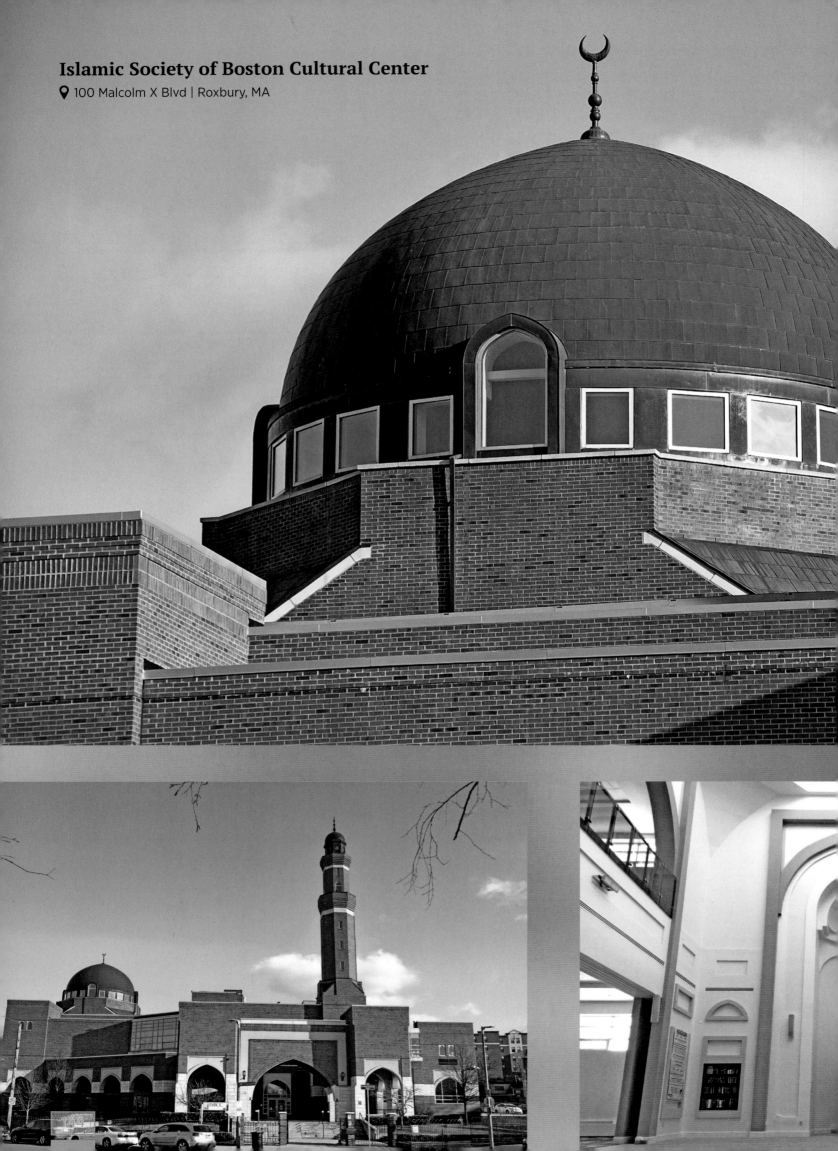

Islamic Society of Boston Cultural Center
100 Malcolm X Blvd | Roxbury, MA

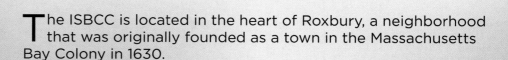

The ISBCC is located in the heart of Roxbury, a neighborhood that was originally founded as a town in the Massachusetts Bay Colony in 1630.

The $17 million, 65,000 square foot structure sits on a two-acre lot. Construction started in December 2004 and was inaugurated in August 2008.

The structure is adorned by a minaret covered in copper that extends 120 feet in the air and a thirty-five foot diameter dome that is also covered in copper. The exterior is made of brick and copper to match the traditional buildings in the city of Boston. There are many recessed areas in the exterior and interior facades filled with Islamic ornaments and calligraphies.

The building has a fifty-car garage in the basement.

American Moslem Society

9945 Vernor Hwy | Dearborn, MI

The American Moslem Society mosque was established in 1938. It is the oldest mosque in the state of Michigan. It has evolved from a small house to a building that occupies 48,000 square feet. In 1952, the AMS along with community members decided to launch the second expansion which doubled the size of the mosque. It increased from a few thousand to 12,000 square feet. In 1986, the community again decided to expand the mosque. The size of the building doubled from 12,000 to 24,000 square feet. In 1982, the weekend school was added.

Islamic Center of America

📍 19500 Ford Rd | Dearborn, MI

Albanian Islamic Center

📍 19775 Harper Ave | Harper Woods, MI

The Albanian Islamic Center, built in Harper Woods in 1963, boasts a distinctive Balkan-style dome and minaret. The Center's founder and first imam, Vehbi Ismail, came to Detroit in 1949 and established the Albanian American Moslem Society in the same year. He was an active Muslim leader who worked vigorously to end communist rule in Albania and guarantee religious freedom for its citizens.

Islamic Center of Saginaw

📍 4330 N Center Rd | Saginaw, MI

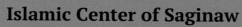

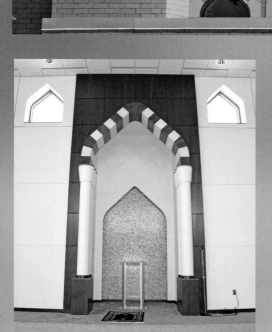

Dar-Ul-Islam Masjid

📍 517 Weidman Rd | Ballwin, MO

The Islamic Foundation of Greater St Louis, Inc. (IFGSTL) was established in 1974.

This masjid can accommodate 1,000 worshippers in the main hall. The women's prayer hall can accommodate about 500.

Islamic Center of Central Missouri

📍 201 S 5th St | Columbia, MO

The Islamic Center of Central Missouri was established in 1983 as a mosque and community center for the central Missouri region.

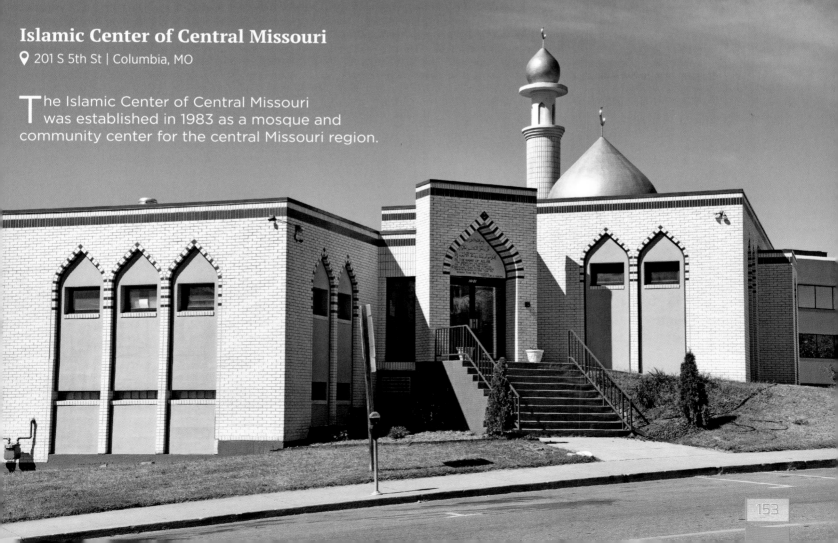

Islamic Society of Greater Kansas City

📍 8501 E 99th St | Kansas City, MO

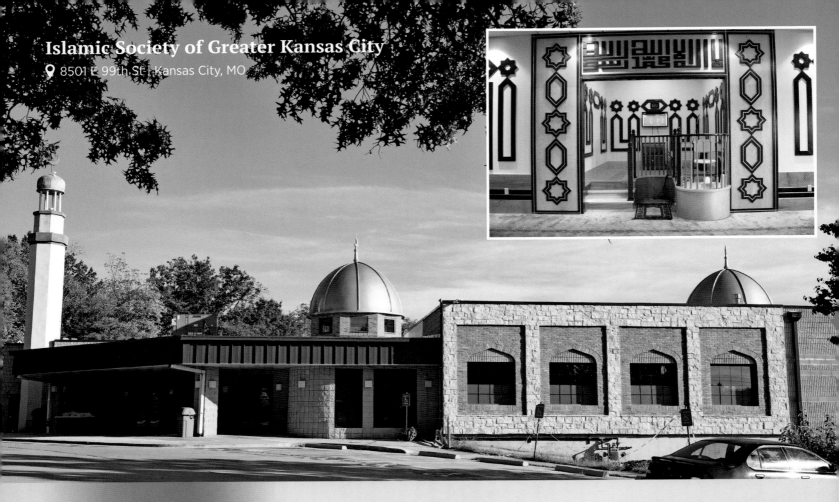

In the early 1970s, the small Muslim community in Kansas City gathered to hold the first Salah (prayer) for Eid al-Fitr. A few years later, four acres of land were purchased, and a mosque was constructed. This mosque opened its doors in March 1981.

In December 1981, the community purchased nine acres of land for a community park. They also established a school, the Madrasat Anoor (School of Light), that year. In May 1984, through a joint project with the Islamic Society of Central Missouri in Columbia, the community purchased nine acres for a Muslim cemetery. In 1987, a full-time Islamic school opened in the center. The center housed the school until a new school building was constructed in August 1997, on four acres of adjacent land.

Rolla Masjid

📍 1302 N Elm St | Rolla, MO

St. Louis Islamic Center

9528 Reavis Barracks Rd | St. Louis, MO

Jamia Masjid

📍 4730 E Desert Inn Rd | Las Vegas, NV

The Islamic Society of Nevada, founded in 1975 by a handful of students, has its roots in the Muslim Student Association. In 1986 an apartment duplex was donated to the society by a local doctor for prayer purposes.

In 1993, the first phase of the construction of the mosque began and the first Jumma prayers happened in the mosque on the last Friday of Ramadan that year.

In 1995, a school building was added to the mosque. The school attracted almost 150 students by the end of 1996.

Donated by the Shaikh Zahid family, the school consists of nine classrooms, a library, two bathrooms, a reception area, a social hall with a seating capacity of 500 people, and a commercial kitchen.

In 2003, the mosque further expanded and added a mezzanine floor with facilities for women.

The mosque can now accommodate over 1000 people.

Masjid Al-Wali

📍 10 Olsen Ave | Edison, NJ

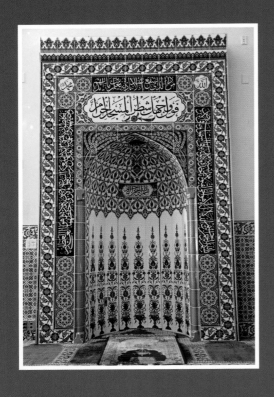

On December 12, 2011, a contract to purchase the property at 10 Olsen Ave in Edison, NJ was signed, and on March 29, 2012, the deal was closed. Documents were signed, and purchase of the property was completed.

The plans and drawings were submitted to Edison Township for approval to begin the construction phase on August 5, 2012. It wasn't until almost a year later that the construction permits were received, and a groundbreaking ceremony took place took on May 17, 2013. Several religious and political leaders attended.

It took until October 2013 for construction to really get started, and on June 26, 2014, the masjid opened up just in time for Ramadan.

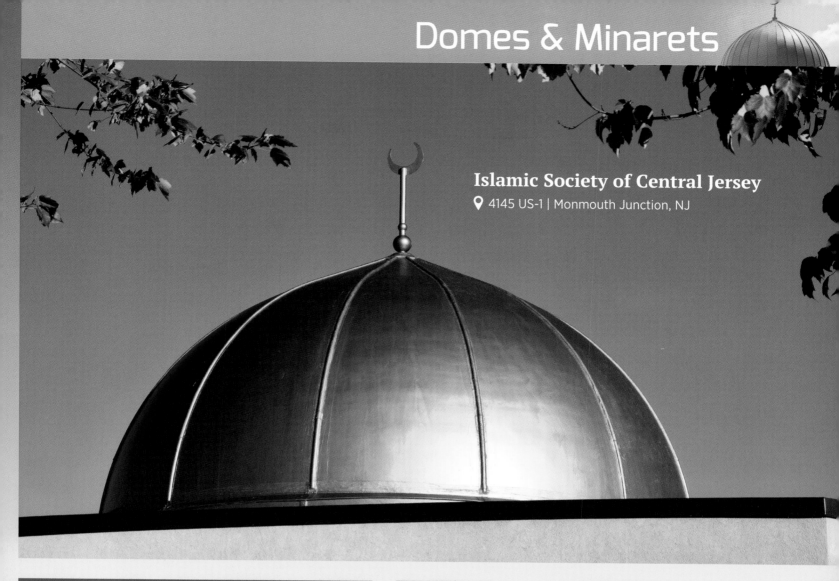

Domes & Minarets

Islamic Society of Central Jersey
📍 4145 US-1 | Monmouth Junction, NJ

Islamic Center of Passaic County
📍 152 Derrom Ave | Paterson, NJ

Masjidulllah Plainfield
📍 321 Grant Ave | Plainfield, NJ

Masjid-e-Ali

📍 47 Cedar Grove Ln | Somerset, NJ

The foundation of Masjid-e-Ali (may Allah be pleased with him) was laid on September 9, 2006. The inauguration ceremony took place on November 20th, 2010.

Darul Islah

320 Fabry Terrace | Teaneck, NJ

Alnaser Masjid

📍 383 Oldham Rd | Wayne, NJ

Dar Al-Islam

📍 342 County Rd 155 | Abiquiu, NM

Dar al-Islam was the first planned Islamic community in the United States. It was originally co-founded in 1979 by Nooruddeen Durkee, an American convert to Islam; Sahl Kabbani, a Saudi businessman; and Abdullah Naseef, the former secretary-general of the World Muslim League. Kabbani reportedly contributed $125 thousand to the non-profit Lama Foundation that was formed to create the community, while the bulk of the start-up funds were said to have come from the Riyadh Ladies' Benevolent Association of Saudi Arabia, the

Masjid Al-Huda

📍 1621 County Rd 155 | Abiquiu, NM

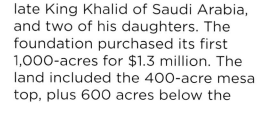

late King Khalid of Saudi Arabia, and two of his daughters. The foundation purchased its first 1,000-acres for $1.3 million. The land included the 400-acre mesa top, plus 600 acres below the mesa – a lush, fertile tract along the Chama River. The masjid and school were designed by the Egyptian architect Hassan Fathy and were constructed of mud bricks (adobe). The main buildings were completed in 1981, and Dar al-Islam opened in 1982.

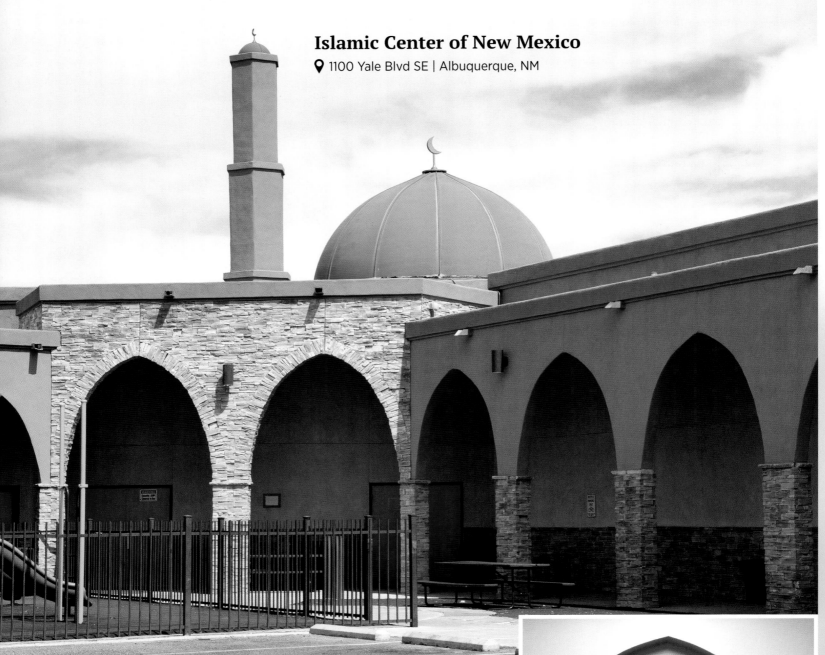

Islamic Center of New Mexico

📍 1100 Yale Blvd SE | Albuquerque, NM

The first Muslims who arrived in Albuquerque in the early 70s began their Juma' service at the University of New Mexico Chapel. Later they moved to the back of a Muslim businessman's store.

The first mosque/Islamic center opened its doors in Albuquerque in December 1986. About twenty years later, in October 2006, a new and expanded mosque/center was built to meet the growing needs of the community.

The Golden Mosque

900 Mitchell Rd | Clovis, NM

The Golden Mosque

THE GOLDEN MOSQUE

Gallup Islamic Center

3100 SR-118 | Gallup, NM

Masjid Al-Huda

📍 1065 E Boutz Rd | Las Cruces, NM

Masjid Al-Huda was established just north of the campus of New Mexico State University (NMSU) in Las Cruces in 1999. Its beautiful architecture is modeled after the Dome of the Rock in Jerusalem; the eight-sided structure has a minaret and a gold dome. Prior to establishing the center, Muslims used to gather in local homes or commute to Phoenix mosques for Friday prayers.

Masjid Khadijah
📍 507 Ranchitos Rd | Taos, NM

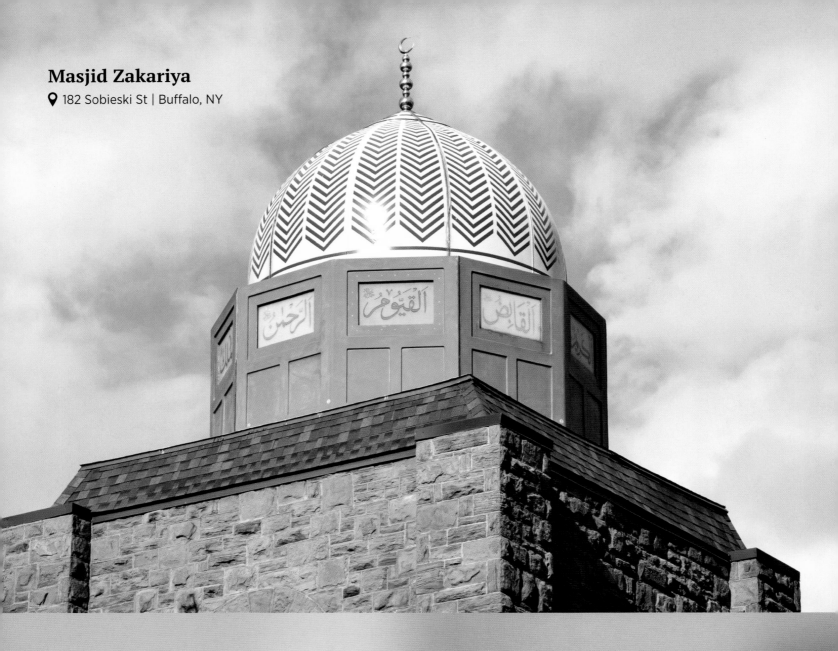

Masjid Zakariya

📍 182 Sobieski St | Buffalo, NY

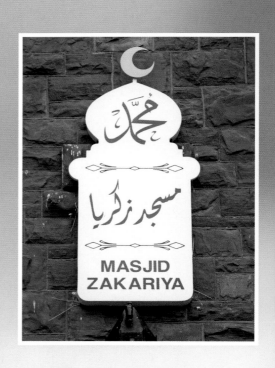

Jaffarya Islamic Center

📍 10300 Transit Rd | East Amherst, NY

Masjidi Hazrati Abu Bakr Siddique

📍 141-47 33rd Ave | Flushing, NY

Middletown Islamic Center

📍 169 Ryerson Rd | New Hampton, NY

Islamic Cultural Center of New York

📍 1711 3rd Ave | New York, NY

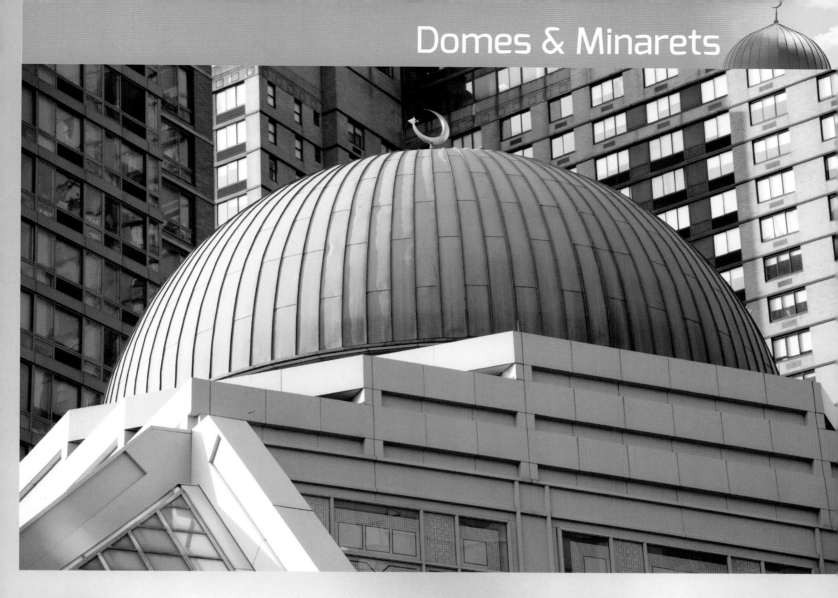

Plans for a large Islamic center in New York were originally drawn up in the late 1960s. The first center started functioning on a small scale from a modest townhouse at 1 Riverside Drive by 72nd Street.

Construction of the Islamic Cultural Center began in October 1984 and construction of the associated mosque began on May 28, 1987. The cornerstone of the minaret was laid on September 26, 1988. The mosque officially opened on April 15, 1991.

More than forty-six Muslim countries made contributions toward the $17 million construction cost.

Source: wikipedia.org

Islamic Center of Long Island

📍 835 Brush Hollow Rd | Westbury, NY

Islamic Center of Long Island

The idea of the Islamic Center of Long Island grew out of the concerns of a small group of Muslim families, mostly immigrants who settled in Nassau County in the early 70s. ICLI was incorporated as a non-profit entity in April 1982 (Rajab 1402) under the provisions of the Religious Corporation Law.

The property for their masjid was purchased in 1984 at 835 Brush Hollow Road.

Construction for the present structure began in July 1989 and was completed in 1991 at a cost of approximately $2 million.

The center comprises of a mosque, with its inspiring prayer room featuring traditional Islamic architecture set in a modern American context, a library, classrooms, and offices totaling an area of approximately 10,000 square feet.

Islamic Center of Rochester

The Islamic Center of Rochester was established in 1975.

The new building of the Islamic Center of Rochester was completed in 1985. it is located on four acres of prime land within ten minutes of downtown Rochester and the major universities and colleges in the area. It has over 8,000 square feet of floor space, which includes prayer and multipurpose halls, offices, a library, and a kitchen. There is a picnic shed adjacent to a pond for summer recreation.

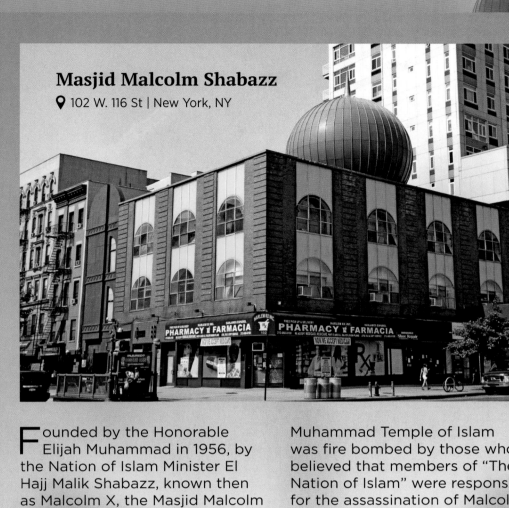

Masjid Malcolm Shabazz
📍 102 W. 116 St | New York, NY

Founded by the Honorable Elijah Muhammad in 1956, by the Nation of Islam Minister El Hajj Malik Shabazz, known then as Malcolm X, the Masjid Malcolm Shabazz located at 102 West 116th Street in Harlem began as Muhammad's Temple of Islam #7.

On February 21, 1965, the Muhammad Temple of Islam was fire bombed by those who believed that members of "The Nation of Islam" were responsible for the assassination of Malcolm X.

In 1976, Imam W. D. Mohammed renamed Muhammad's Temple of Islam #7 as Masjid Malcolm Shabazz.

Islamic Center of Rochester
📍 727 Westfall Rd | Rochester, NY

Noor Islamic Cultural Center

📍 5001 Wilcox Rd | Dublin, OH

"The commanding white structure sits on the edge of cornfields in the suburbs, striking in design yet puzzling in its purpose. One of the largest new Islamic worship centers in the US doesn't look like a mosque, at least at first glance." Paul Vernon, AP

The Noor Center was designed with two side domes with a diameter of fourteen feet, and no minaret. The 38,000 square foot facility over seven acres of land cost $7.4 million and was inaugurated in 2006.

Islamic Center of Cleveland

📍 6055 W 130th St | Parma, OH

Islamic Center of Greater Toledo

25877 Scheider Rd | Perrysburg, OH

OHIO
HISTORICAL
MARKER

ISLAMIC CENTER OF GREATER TOLEDO

The first Muslim immigrants arrived in the 1900s from Syria and Lebanon. They established the Syrian American Muslim Society in the late 1930s. In 1954, the first Islamic Center was built on East Bancroft Street. By the late 60s and early 70s, the growing Muslim community outgrew the Bancroft Street Center. The present Center, architecturally classic in Islamic style, was the first such mosque in North America. Its foundation was laid in October 1980 and was officially opened on October 22, 1983. In August 2001, the full time Islamic School of Greater Toledo opened. Today, the Center's members represent nearly 30 nationalities, providing an important bridge of understanding between its members and the community at large.

THE OHIO BICENTENNIAL COMMISSION
THE ISLAMIC CENTER OF GREATER TOLEDO
THE OHIO HISTORICAL SOCIETY
2003   42-48

Masjid An-Nasr

📍 3815 N St Clair Ave | Oklahoma City, OK

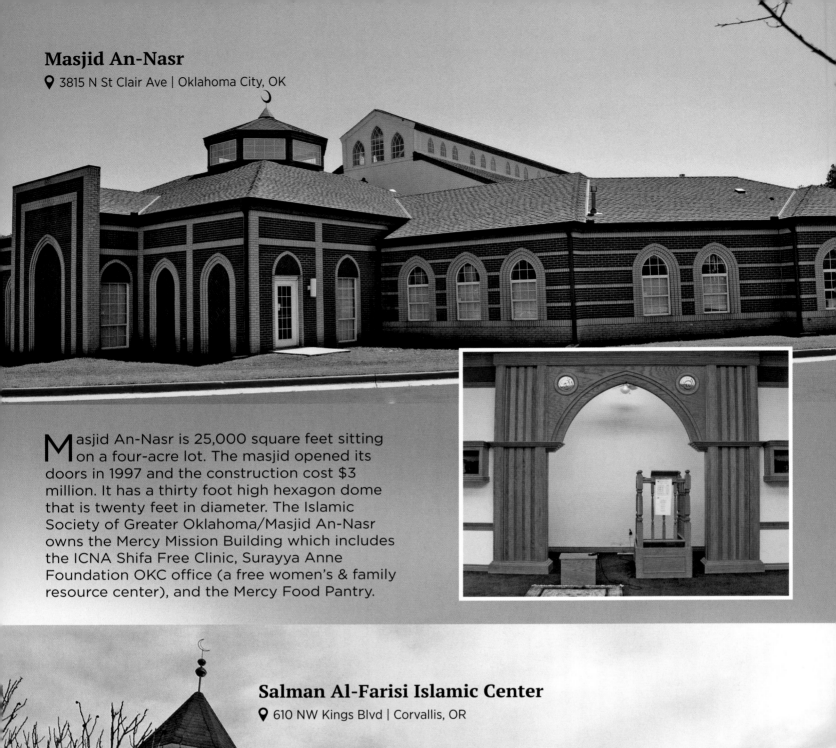

Masjid An-Nasr is 25,000 square feet sitting on a four-acre lot. The masjid opened its doors in 1997 and the construction cost $3 million. It has a thirty foot high hexagon dome that is twenty feet in diameter. The Islamic Society of Greater Oklahoma/Masjid An-Nasr owns the Mercy Mission Building which includes the ICNA Shifa Free Clinic, Surayya Anne Foundation OKC office (a free women's & family resource center), and the Mercy Food Pantry.

Salman Al-Farisi Islamic Center

📍 610 NW Kings Blvd | Corvallis, OR

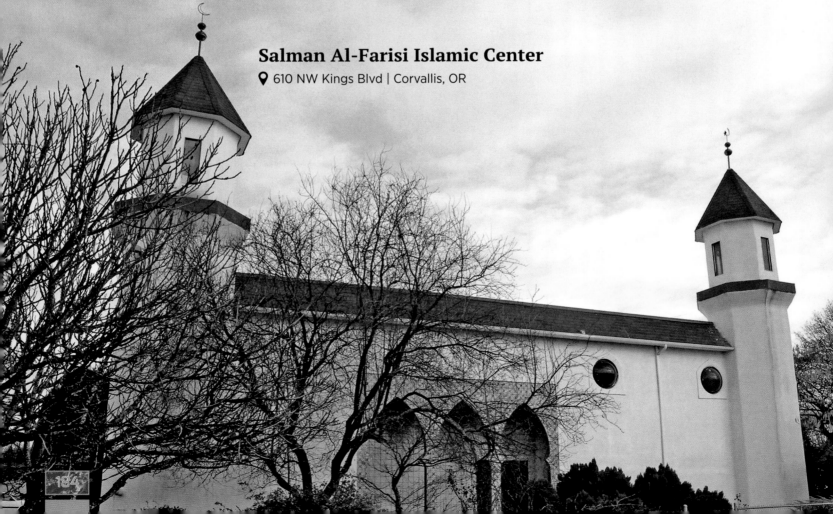

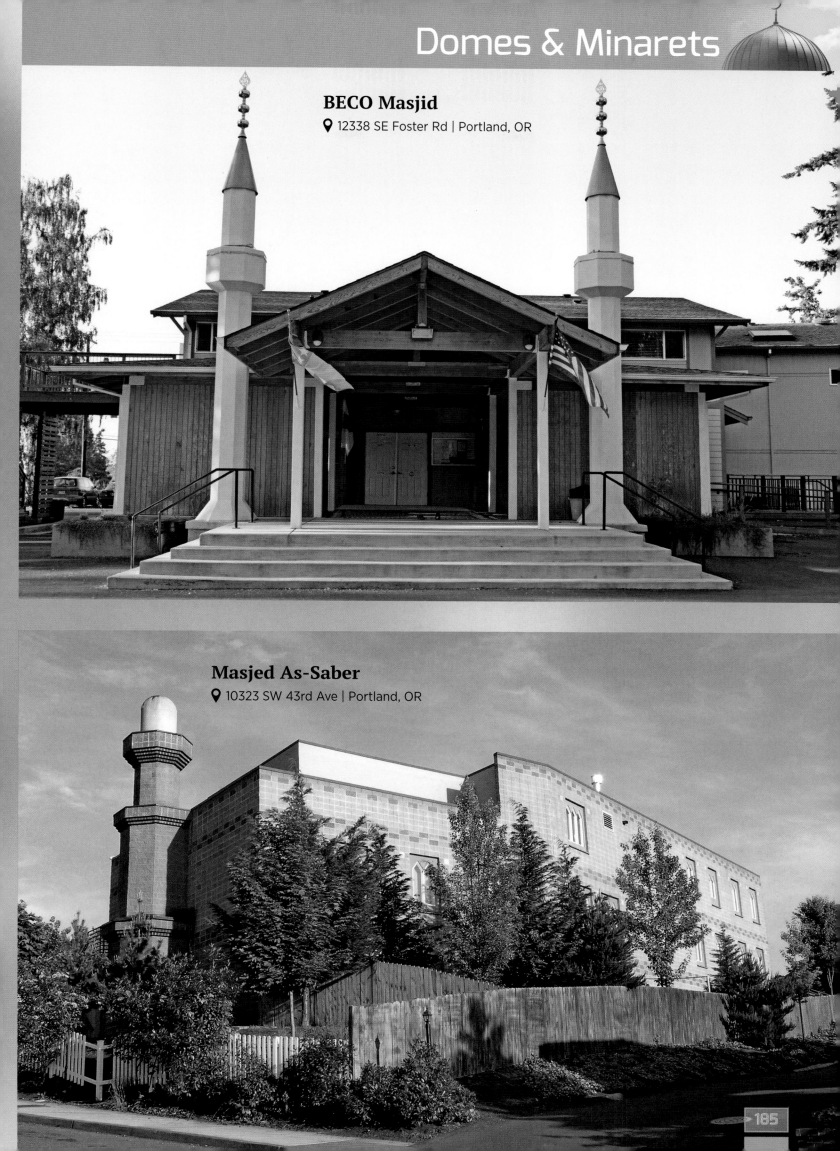

BECO Masjid
📍 12338 SE Foster Rd | Portland, OR

Masjed As-Saber
📍 10323 SW 43rd Ave | Portland, OR

Islamic Center of Hatillo

Carrizales (Intersection of Cll & Cll Jade) | Hatillo, Puerto Rico

Islamic Center of Fajardo
📍 Calle A Nte. | Fajardo, Puerto Rico

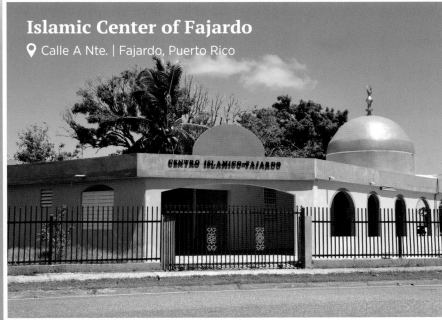

In 2007, there were over 5,000 Muslims residing in Puerto Rico. The early Muslim community largely consisted mainly of Palestinian and Jordanian immigrants who arrived between 1958 and 1962. A storefront mosque on Calle Padre Colón in the Río Piedras district of San Juan served the entire religious community on the island during earlier years, however, today there are mosques and Islamic centers in Aguadilla, Hatillo, Fajardo, Ponce, Vega Alta, and San Juan. The American Muslim Association of North America (AMANA) also has an office in Cayey.

Source: wikipedia.org

Masjid Othman Ibn Affan
📍 29 Luna St | Ponce, Puerto Rico

Masjid Al-Faruq
📍 Calle Caiman | Vega Alta, Puerto Rico

Masjid Al-Islam

📍 40 Sayles Hill Rd | North Smithfield, RI

Masjid Annour

📍 2533 Gunbarrel Rd | Chattanooga, TN

Islamic Ctr of Murfreesboro

📍 2605 Veals Rd | Murfreesboro, TN

Started in 1982, the Islamic Center of Murfreesboro (ICM) was incorporated in 1997. In October 2003, ICM purchased a small plaza and occupied a building of 21,000 square feet near Middle Tennessee State University. In 2009, the group purchased an area of undeveloped land. At the time, Ground Zero mosque controversies were prevalent in the United States and after a series of litigations, attacks against the ICM and Muslim community, and a federal intervention, the building opened on August 10, 2012 for Friday prayers. The mosque received its permanent certificate of occupancy on August 23, 2012. The litigation against the mosque's opening finally came to an end on June 2, 2014.

There were only a handful of Muslims in Nashville in 1979 when the ICN purchased an old house in 1979 on the corner of 12th Avenue and Sweetbriar Street with a collection of $30,000 and a generous donation from Yusuf Islam (Cat Stevens). In 1989, the old house was demolished and a new mosque was built. In 1995, the ICN bought a 10.6-acre plot of land on Charlotte Pike near exit 199 off I-40 West. The ICN also purchased land for a Muslim graveyard and established a full-time Islamic school in 1995. On December 1, 2008, the first phase of the new school building was completed and opened, providing education for students from Pre-K thru 6th grades.

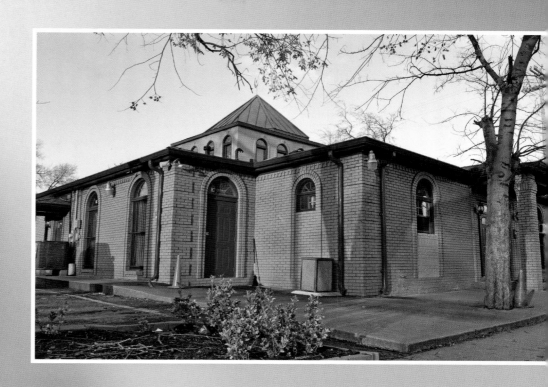

Islamic Center of Nashville

📍 2515 12th Ave S | Nashville, TN

Islamic Center of El Paso

📍 143 Paragon Ln | El Paso, TX

Masjid Al-Ibrahimi
📍 4901 Diaz Ave | Ft. Worth, TX

1974 witnessed the first Eid celebration by local Muslims in an apartment complex in the Fort Worth area. A few years later, in 1977, the Islamic Association of Tarrant County was officially registered. The group purchased land in 1978 and the masjid was built in 1981. In April 1996, the Ar-Rawdah Cemetery was completed. The groundbreaking ceremony for Masjid Al-Ibrahimee took place in 2002 on 6.2 acres of land that had been donated six years earlier. The masjid was inaugurated in 2005.

Masjid Al-Hedayah
📍 8601 Randol Mill Rd | Ft. Worth, TX

Makkah Masjid

3301 W Buckingham Rd | Garland, TX

Islamic Society of Greater Houston (ISGH-Main)

📍 3110 Eastside St | Houston, TX

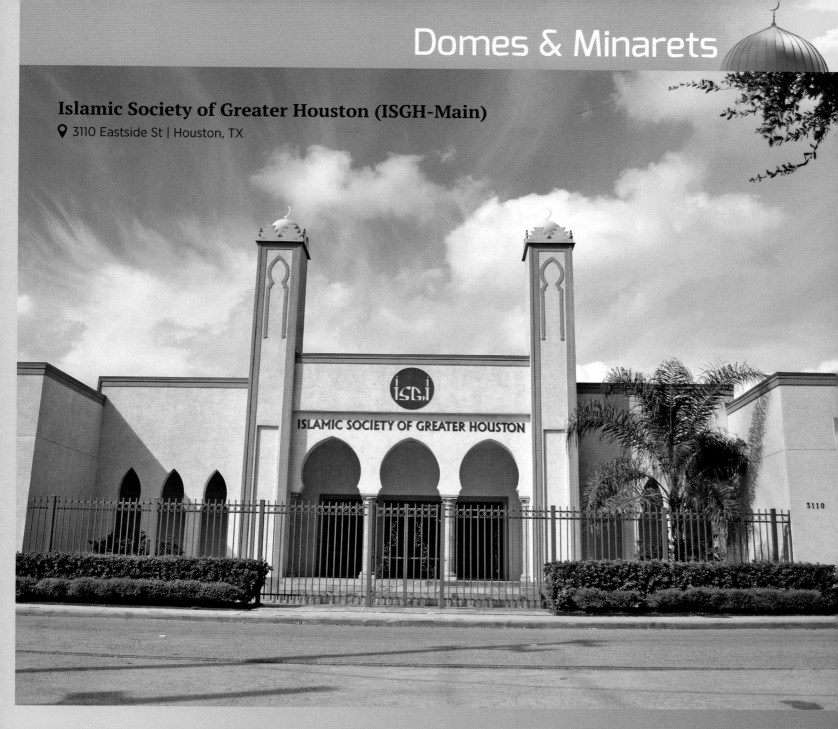

The Islamic Society of Greater Houston (ISGH) was established in 1969 in the heart of the city of Houston. The first Eid was prayed in the house of one of the founders of the society. ISGH now represents twenty-one communities from all over the greater Houston area.

Masjid Al-Rasul

📍 9300 S Course Dr | Houston, TX

Masjid Warithud-deen Mohammed

📍 6641 Bellfort Ave | Houston, TX

Houston Masjid of Al-Islam was founded in the 1950s in the barbershop of Charlie Boyd and was Houston's oldest and most historic Muslim Community.

It began as Temple #45 of the Nation of Islam.

A former Christian Scientist Church was purchased with funds donated by heavyweight champion Muhammad Ali and converted into a masjid, which remained the home of the Houston Masjid of Al-Islam until the building was destroyed by Hurricane Ike in September 2008.

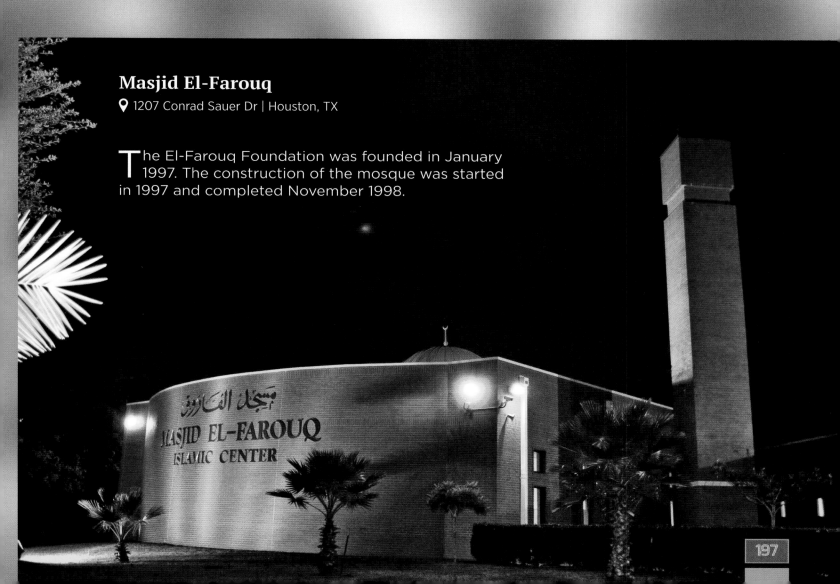

Masjid El-Farouq

📍 1207 Conrad Sauer Dr | Houston, TX

The El-Farouq Foundation was founded in January 1997. The construction of the mosque was started in 1997 and completed November 1998.

Islamic Center of Irving

📍 2555 Esters Rd | Irving, TX

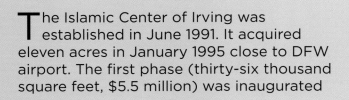

The Islamic Center of Irving was established in June 1991. It acquired eleven acres in January 1995 close to DFW airport. The first phase (thirty-six thousand square feet, $5.5 million) was inaugurated on April 30, 2005. The second phase (thirty-nine thousand square feet, $6 million) that planned to add a gym and a house for the Islamic School of Irving started in 1995 and completed in 2016.

The Islamic Center of the South Plains incorporated in 1981 and purchased land in 1982. The masjid was built in 1985 and expanded in 1996. Additional land was purchased, and a community hall was added in 1999. To serve the student community more effectively, the student cultural center (student mosque) was built in 2008.

Islamic Center of the South Plains

📍 3419 La Salle Ave | Lubbock, TX

East Plano Islamic Center

 1350 Star Ct | Plano, TX

Pearland Islamic Center (ISGH-Southeast)

 1530 Garden Rd | Pearland, TX

The East Plano Islamic Center (EPIC) started in 2003 in a trailer house. The EPIC master plan was drawn to contain a masjid and business offices. In 2008, the offices were completed and used as a temporary musalla. Seven years later, the current masjid compound was inaugurated for Ramadan.

The 79,500 square foot compound (33,700 square foot main prayer building, 35,800 square foot extension, and 10,000 square foot waqf area) was built on 10.1 acres of land and cost $15 million. The outside structure of the masjid has one dome that is fifty-five feet high and twenty-eight feet in diameter.

Plano Masjid

📍 6401 Independence Pkwy | Plano, TX

The Islamic Association of Collin County (IACC) was established in 1991. Members rented a small facility located on the third floor of a shopping center that accommodated a maximum of fifty people to hold regular prayers. In 1995, the community grew exponentially and IACC membership exceeded over 1,000 families. A new facility was leased at the intersection of Parker and Custer Road to keep up with the demand for services. In 1997, the strategic planning committee initiated the construction of a new community center and IACC purchased 4.59 acres of land at the intersection of Spring Creek and Independence Parkway. IACC raised over $2 million to support the construction of a new 12,000 square foot community center.

Dallas Central Mosque
📍 840 Abrams Rd | Richardson, TX

The Islamic Association of North Texas (IANT) was established in February 1971. What started in a small house in the early 1970s in Grand Prairie and moved to a bigger house in 1979 on Abrams Street in Richardson, evolved to be the main organization on the east side of the Dallas/Fort Worth area until the early part of the 2000s. The masjid with a magnificent dome and minaret was opened in 1985 and expanded to become an 80,000 square foot facility by the late 1990s. With the massive relocation of Muslims to the Dallas/Fort Worth area, several new organizations grew out of IANT such as the Islamic Association of Collin County and the East Plano Islamic Center and became just as big in a very short period of time.

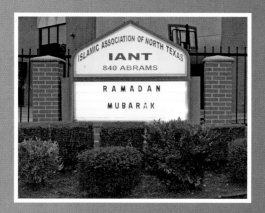

Masjid Maryam (ISGH-Southwest)

504 Sartartia Rd | Sugar Land, TX

Victoria Islamic Center

📍 201 E Airline Rd | Victoria, TX

In 1991, the Victoria Islamic Center was officially organized by the founding members.

As the Muslim population grew, land at 201 E. Airline Road in Victoria was purchased for the construction of the masjid. It took several more years to acquire enough funds to build the masjid on these grounds with the formal grand opening in May 2000.

The masjid was destroyed by an arson fire in the early morning hours of January 28, 2017.

Mosque Maryam

📍 425 N 700 W | Salt Lake City, UT

Mustafa Center

📍 6844 Braddock Rd | Annandale, VA

The Mustafa Center was established by the Afghan Academy with the support of local Muslims. In 1995, a 7,800 square foot abandoned property was purchased. Construction began in September 1997. After a little more than two years, the Mustafa Center was officially opened (November 1999). The total cost of the land and construction was well over $1 million.

The Mustafa Center's exterior features a light-green dome, two domed minarets on each side, and an arch entrance portico supported by columns and tiles with Quranic inscriptions. The interior is adorned with beautiful chandeliers and a lovely mihrab.

The Mustafa Center has two floors. The upper floor is the musalla with separate sections for men and women. The lower floor consists of an office, classrooms, library, gathering hall, and restrooms.

Islamic Center Northern Virginia

📍 4420 Shirley Gate Rd | Fairfax, VA

Dar Al Hijrah Islamic Center

📍 3159 Row St | Falls Church, VA

Dar Al-Hijrah is a strong community with approximately 40,000 Muslims residing in the area that the center serves. For approximately eight years, the original masjid for this group was a house that remains on the premises.

Construction of the current facility began in 1986 and despite seemingly insurmountable obstacles, the facility was opened on March 2, 1991.

Mosque and Islamic Center of Hampton Roads

📍 22 Tide Mill Ln | Hampton, VA

The construction of the mosque was completed in 1983. The official opening was on April 21, 1984 and was attended by a state delegate, the mayors of Hampton and Newport News, Virginia, and various civic and military leaders from the area. The mosque was the first in the state of Virginia that had Islamic architecture.

Masjid Umar Al-Farooq

5507 238th St SW | Mountlake Terrace, WA

Domes & Minarets

Islamic Center of Tri-Cities

📍 2900 Bombing Range Rd | West Richland, WA

A small residential house was initially purchased in 1986 to serve the needs of fifteen Muslim families. Later, the community outgrew that place as they expanded to 100 families. They decided to buy 2.5 acres of land and built the present mosque in 1996. The mosque currently serves more than 500 families along with almost 1500 Muslims living in the tri-cities area.

Muslim Association of Huntington
📍 944 20th St | Huntington, WV

Albanian Islamic Center
📍 6001 88th Ave | Kenosha, WI

Iman Mosque

📍 4707 S 13th St | Milwaukee, WI

The Islamic Society of Milwaukee was established on July 16, 1976. The 60,000 square foot structure with two minarets and one dome sits on a seven-acre lot. It was opened on July 1, 1982.

Masjid As-Siddiq | South Ozone Park, NY

Al-Ahad Islamic Center | Allentown, PA

Mosque of San Gibriel | San Gabriel, CA

Colleyville Masjid | Colleyville, TX

East Texas Islamic Center | Tyler, TX

Masjid Al-Ansaar | Conroe, TX

Masjid Al-Qubbatu Al-Khadra | Pelham, AL

Darul Arqum Islamic Center | Ames, IA

Islamic Ctr of Conejo Valley | Newbury Park, CA

Nur-Ul-Islam Masjid | Cooper City, FL

Masjid Al-Madeenah | Springfield, OH

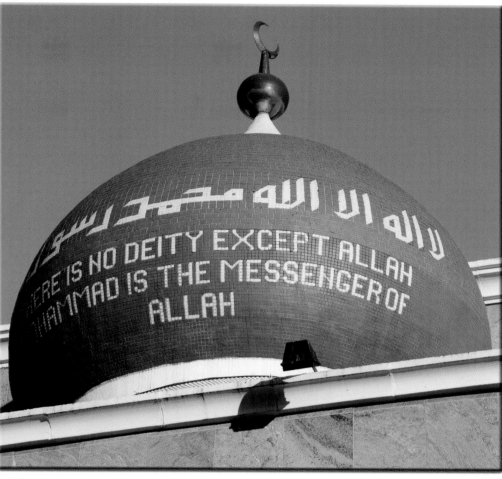

Muslim Center of New York | Flushing, NY

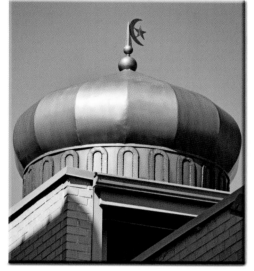

Parkchester Jame Masjid | Bronx, NY

Makki Masjid | Chicago, IL

Islamic Ctr of Elizabethtown
Elizabethtown, KY

Imam Ali Center | Woodside, NY

Masjid Al-Hikmah | Astoria, NY

Long Beach Islamic Center | Signal Hill, CA

Islamic Ctr of St. Joseph | St. Joseph, MO

219

Masjid Maamor
Jamaica, NY

Masjid Jamaat-ul-Muttaqeen
Pembroke Pines, FL

Madera Masjid | Madera, CA

Masjid An-Nur | Minneapolis, MN

Masjid Ar-Rahmah | Redmond, WA

Islamic Center of Boca Raton
Boca Raton, FL

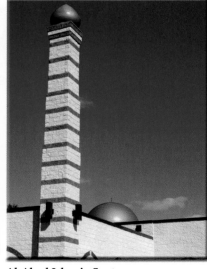

Al-Ahad Islamic Center
Allentown, PA

Islamic Center of Brownsville | Brownsville, TX

La Mirada Masjid | La Mirada, CA

Islamic Center of Tucson
Tucson, AZ

Imam Al-Khoei Foundation
Jamaica, NY

Fiji Jamaat-Ul Islam of America | South San Francisco, CA

Masjid Al-Noor | Bakersfield, CA

Islamic Community Center of Augusta
Augusta, GA

Albanian American Islamic Center
Glendale, NY

Islamic Center of Yuma
Yuma, AZ

Masjid of Antelope Valley
Palmdale, CA

Selimiye Mosque
Methuen, MA

Makkah Learning Center
Gambrills, MD

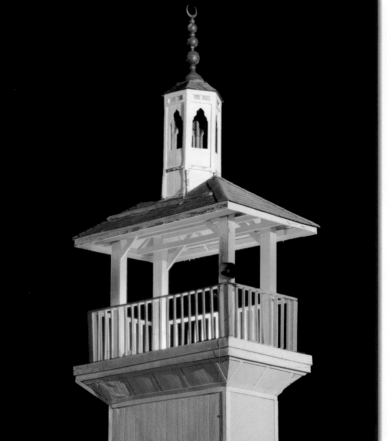

Masjid Al-Tawbah | Charlotte, NC

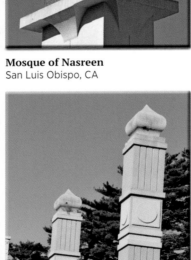

Mosque of Nasreen
San Luis Obispo, CA

Shahid Mosque
Charlotte, NC

Shah E Najaf Center
Brentwood, NY

Albanian American Muslim Comm.
Waterbury, CT

Huntsville Islamic Center
Huntsville, AL

Muslim Society Inc
Glendale Heights, IL

Jamia Al-Karam
Monroe, CT

Alsalaam Mosque
Arvin, CA

Masjid Al-Ikhlas
Newburgh, NY

Islamic Soc. of Greater Lansing
East Lansing, MI

Clear Lake Islamic Center
Clear Lake City, TX

Northwest Islamic Center
St. Louis, MO

Islamic Center of Northwest Florida | Pensacola, FL

Muslim Unity Center
Bloomfield Hills, MI

Masjid Uqbah | Cleveland, OH

Masjid Al Salaam
Rock Hill, SC

Hoover Crescent Islamic Center
Hoover, AL

Al-Rahman Mosque
Rochester, NY

Medina Masjid
St. Louis, MO

Domes & Minarets

Islamic Center of Omaha | Omaha, NE

Masjid Yaseen | Garland, TX

Masjid Al Farouq | Pullman, WA

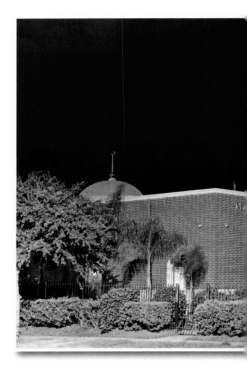
Masjid Uthman Ibn Affan

Islamic Center of Virginia | Richmond, VA

Colleyville Masjid | Colleyville, TX

Annoor Islamic Center | Clemmons, NC

Jefferson City Muslim Community
Jefferson City, MO

Galveston, TX

Islamic Center of Northeast Florida | Jacksonville, FL

Masjid At-Tawheed | Grand Rapids, MI

Masjid Bilal | Cleveland, OH

225

McKinney Islamic Center | McKinney, TX

Islamic Foundation North | Libertyville, IL

Al Khair Mosque | Youngstown, OH

Islamic Cultural Center of Fresno | Fresno, CA

Islamic Center of Hernando County | Spring Hill, FL

Masjid Nur | Port Charlotte, FL

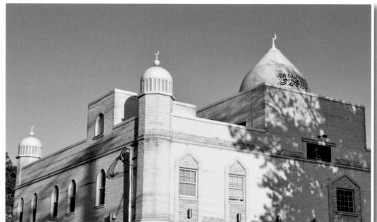

Masjid As-Siddiq | South Ozone Park, NY

Denison Central Mosque | Denison, TX

Islamic Cultural Center Behar | Grand Rapids, MI

Masjid Hamza (ISGH SWZ) | Houston, TX

Islamic Center of South Florida | Pompano Beach, FL

Masjid Ash-Shura

Noori Masjid | Plano, TX

MCECC Masjed | San Anotnio, TX

Islamic Society of Sarasota & Bradenton | Sarasota, FL

Atlanta, GA

Islamic Center of Frisco | Frisco, TX

Oxford Mosque | Oxford, MS

Masjid Al-Noor | Waterloo, IA

Masjid Attaqwa | Sugar Land, TX

Belleville Mosque & Islamic Education Center | Belleville, IL

Islamic Society of Akron and Kent | Cuyahoga Falls, OH

Masjid Darul-Islam of Ocala | Ocala, FL

Islamic Center of Lake City | Lake City, FL

Dar Elsalam Islamic Center | Arlington, TX

Islamic Center of Macomb | Macomb, IL

Islamic Society of Greater Springfield | Springfield, IL

Dar-Us-Sunnah Masjid & Community Center | Evanston, IL

Islamic Center of Corona and Norco | Corona, CA

B&H Islamic Ctr of Pennsylvania | Mechanicsburg, PA

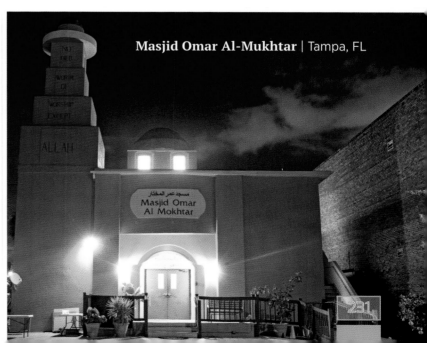

Masjid Omar Al-Mukhtar | Tampa, FL

Until recently, decorations were not part of the structures of mosques in America. There was often a lack of financial and human resources that meant that the focus had to be on the more important things, and decorations weren't a priority. As the Muslim communities started to grow, decorations became more attainable.

The ethnic background of each community influences the decorations and their location. Decorations range in type, complexity, and abundance. They can be Arabic calligraphy of Quranic verses, specific companions' or imams' names, or fancy geometric art. In some mosques, their use is limited to niches only. In others, decorations extend to walls, inside domes, and elsewhere.

Mosque Decoration

King Fahad Mosque

📍 10980 Washington Blvd
Culver City, CA

A few years after starting in a Muslim Student House in West Los Angeles, the Islamic Foundation of Ibn Taymiyah Foundation was incorporated in 1980. The land for a future structure was purchased in 1993.

King Fahad, the late king of Saudi Arabia, pledged funds for the construction of the masjid in 1995.

Following Islamic tradition, there is a marble facade, hand-made tiles from Turkey, and a seventy-two foot high minaret topped with a gold leaf crescent. The minaret is an architectural symbol of Islam.

The structure covers 63,000 square feet and is comprised of a central prayer area, an auditorium, conference rooms, and modern amenities for wudu.

Masjid Abu Bakr Al-Siddiq
📍 29414 Mission Blvd | Hayward, CA

The Islamic Center consists of an 11,000 square foot building with a multipurpose meeting area that is nearly 4,000 square feet.

In January 1985, about seventy-five Muslims, mostly newly-arrived Afghan immigrants, organized the first Friday congregational services (Jumu'ah prayers) and hosted the daily five prayers in a leased storefront on Mission Boulevard.

In May 1988, a three-quarter acre (32,670 square feet) empty lot at 29414 Mission Boulevard was purchased for $260 thousand as location for Hayward's first purpose-built masjid, and in May 1992, Masjid Abu Bakr Al-Siddiq was incorporated. Later, a 2.75-acre parcel of land was bought for $900 thousand for a parking lot.

In June 1996, groundbreaking on a new masjid after an intense $1.6 million fundraising campaign was held and the first phase was completed a year later.

Hatemi Masjid (Anjuman-e-Jamali)

998 San Antonio Rd | Palo Alto, CA

In November 1944, the idea for building a mosque in Washington, DC was born through a discussion between Mr. M. Abu Al Hawa and the former Ambassador of Egypt, Mr. Mahmood Hassan Pasha. Soon thereafter, a handful of diplomats and American Muslims formed the Washington Mosque Foundation. The Foundation's membership quickly grew to include representatives who were American citizens as well as members from every Islamic nation in the world. They all supported the Foundation's appeal for funds and managed to raise enough money to enable them to purchase the land on April 30, 1946. The center is located on Washington's "Embassy Row" the cornerstone was laid on January 11, 1949.

Professor Mario Rossi, a noted Italian architect who built several mosques in Egypt, designed the building. Egypt donated a magnificent bronze chandelier and sent specialists who wrote the Qur'anic verses adorning the mosque's walls and ceiling. The tiles came from Turkey along with the experts to install them. The Persian rugs came from Iran, which are still in the mosque of the center.

Several years later, upon its completion, the Islamic Center of Washington's dedication ceremony took place on June 28, 1957. Former United States President Dwight D. Eisenhower spoke for the American representatives. In his address, he praised the Islamic world's "traditions of learning and rich culture" which have "for centuries contributed to the building of civilization." He affirmed America's founding principle of religious freedom and stated that: "America would fight with her whole strength for your right to have here your own church and worship according to your own conscience. This concept is indeed a part of America, and without that concept we would be something else than what we are."

Eisenhower concluded: "As I stand beneath these graceful arches, sur-rounded on every side by friends from far and near, I am convinced that our common goals are both right and promising. Faithful to the demands of justice and of brotherhood, each working according to the lights of his own conscience, our world must advance along the paths of peace."

Masjidul Islam

📍 1280 Bluff City Blvd | Elgin, IL

The Institute of Islamic Education (IIE) was established in 1989 in Elgin, Illinois.

American Islamic Association

 8860 W St Francis Rd | Frankfort, IL

The American Islamic Association was incorporated in Frankfort, Illinois in 1979.

The fourteen acre scenic property was purchased in 1982, and the mosque was completed in September 2005 at a cost of approximately $2 million generously donated by the South Suburban Muslim community.

Bait Ul Ilm Islamic Center

📍 485 S Bartlett Rd | Streamwood, IL

Diyanet Center of America

9704 Good Luck Rd | Lanham, MD

The Diyanet Center of America (DCA) was established in 1993 by a group of Turkish-Americans. The DCA has twenty-two local chapters with affiliations across America and works in full coordination with the Religious Affairs of the Republic of Turkey (Diyanet). The center cost $110 million. The featured masjid was completed in 2015.

Diyanet Center of America

📍 9704 Good Luck Rd | Lanham, MD

Mosque Decoration

Islamic Society of Boston
📍 204 Prospect St | Cambridge, MA

Selimiye Mosque
📍 105-A Oakland Ave | Methuen, MA

Jam-e-Masjid Islamic Center

📍 110 Harrison St | Boonton, NJ

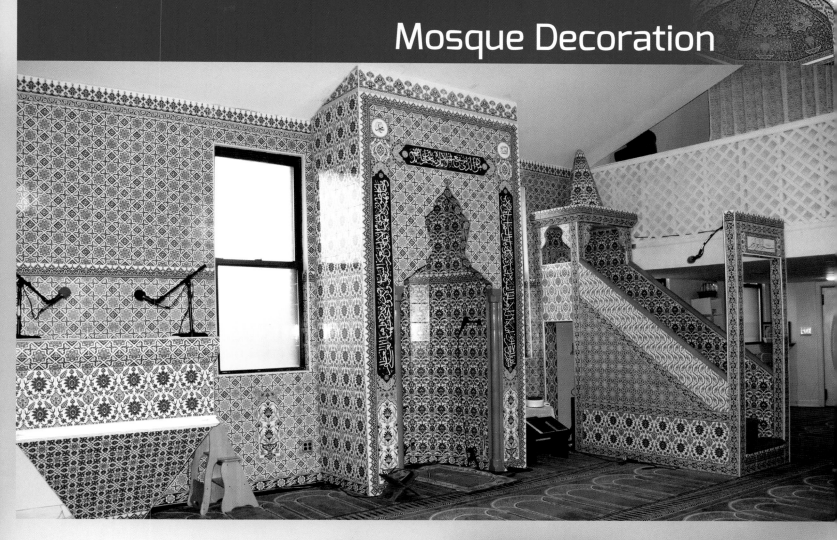

Albanian American Islamic Center

📍 43 Monroe St | Garfield, NJ

Ulu Camii

📍 408 Knickerbocker Ave | Paterson, NJ

Ahmad Samawi Mosque

📍 8092 Plantation Dr | West Chester, OH

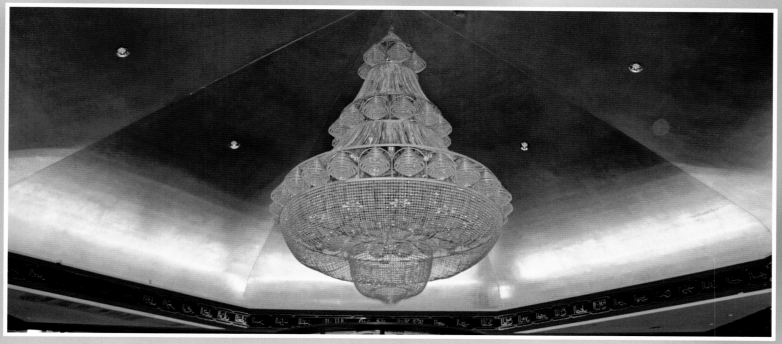

The founding roots of the Islamic Center of Greater Cincinnati (ICGC) goes back to the 1950s when the community purchased a tiny house on Fairview Ave to serve as a masjid. In 1980, they purchased a larger house on Clifton Avenue.

The current ICGC property in West Chester, a 14,000 square foot building, was purchased in 1988 and officially opened in 1995.

255

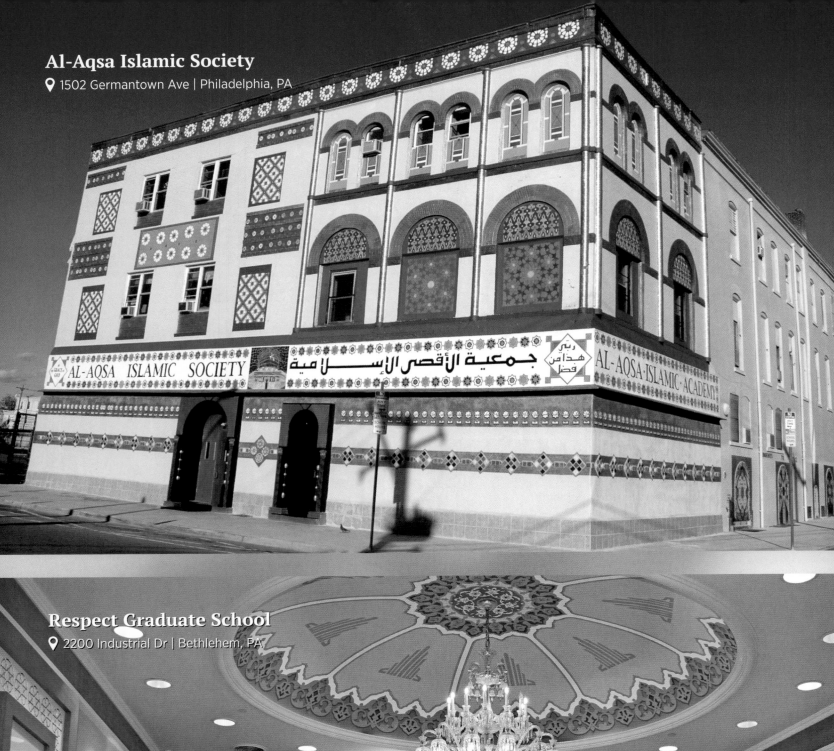

Al-Aqsa Islamic Society

📍 1502 Germantown Ave | Philadelphia, PA

AL-AQSA ISLAMIC SOCIETY

جمعية الأقصى الإسلامية

AL-AQSA-ISLAMIC-ACADEMY

Respect Graduate School

📍 2200 Industrial Dr | Bethlehem, PA

Manassas Mosque

📍 12950 Center Entrance Ct | Manassas, VA

Islamic Center of Shoreline

📍 20001 25th Ave NE | Shoreline, WA

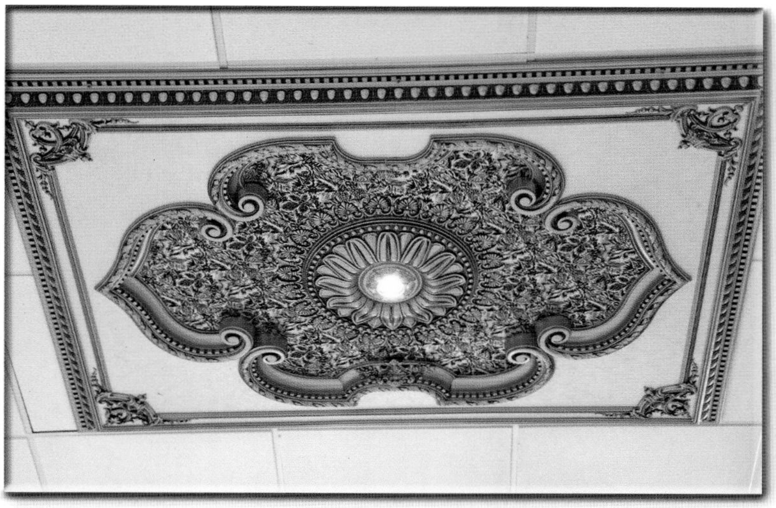

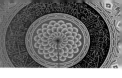

Masjid Al-Jami' | Tampa, FL

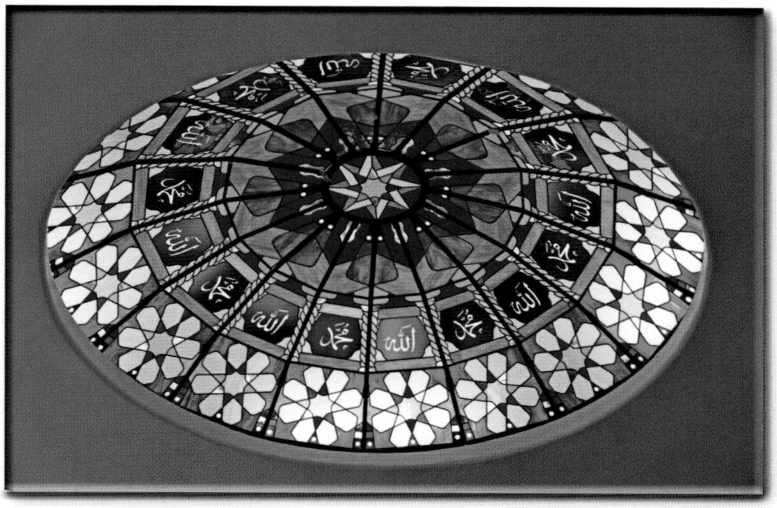

Mission Viejo Masjid | Mission Viejo, CA

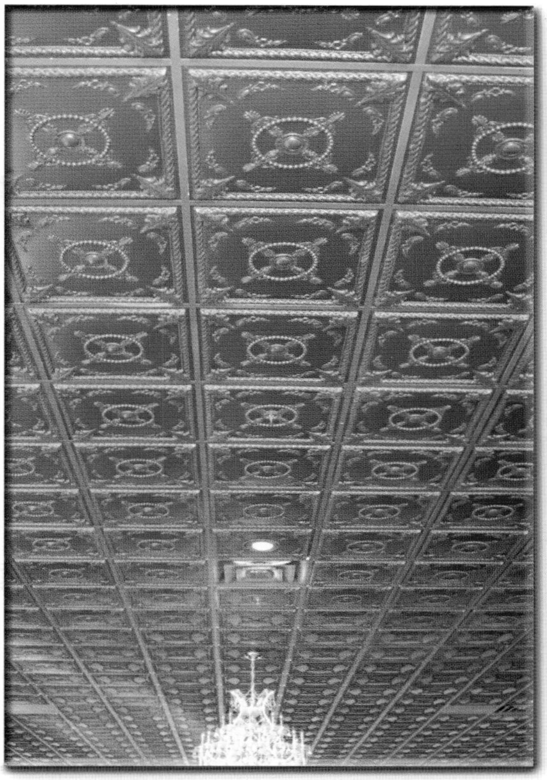

Khursheed Unissa Memorial Com. Ctr
Amarillo, TX

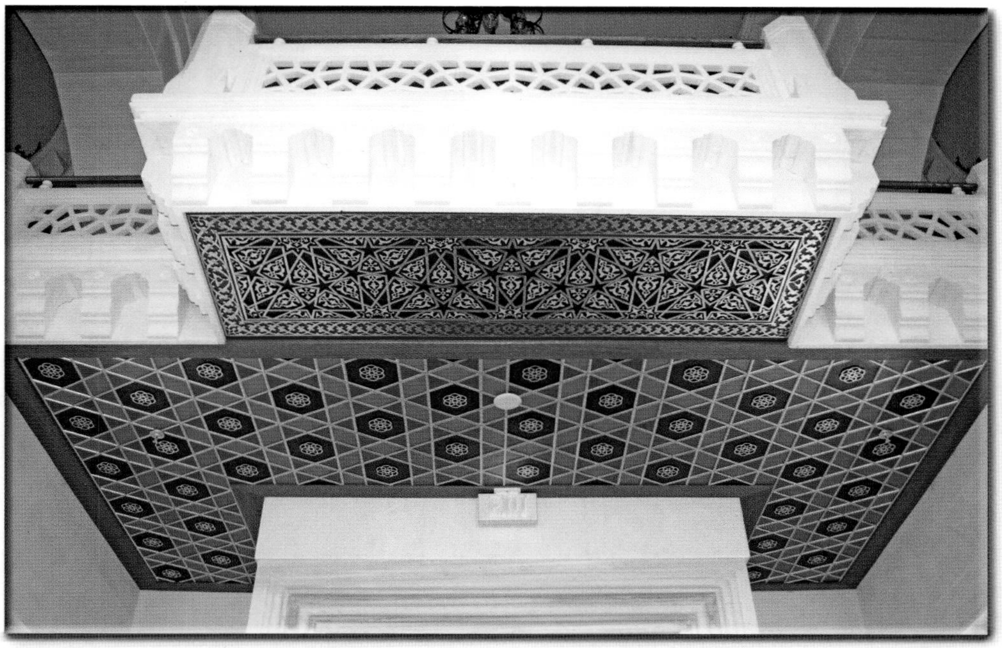

Diyanet Center of America | Lanham, MD

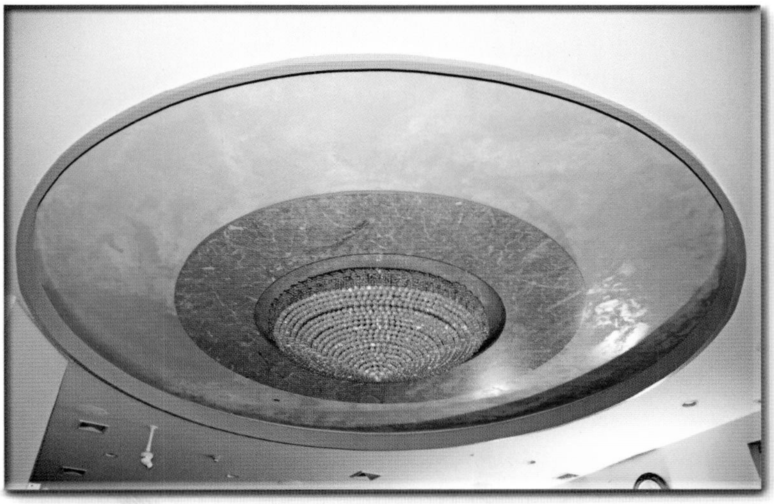

Harlem Islamic Cultural Center | **New York**, NY

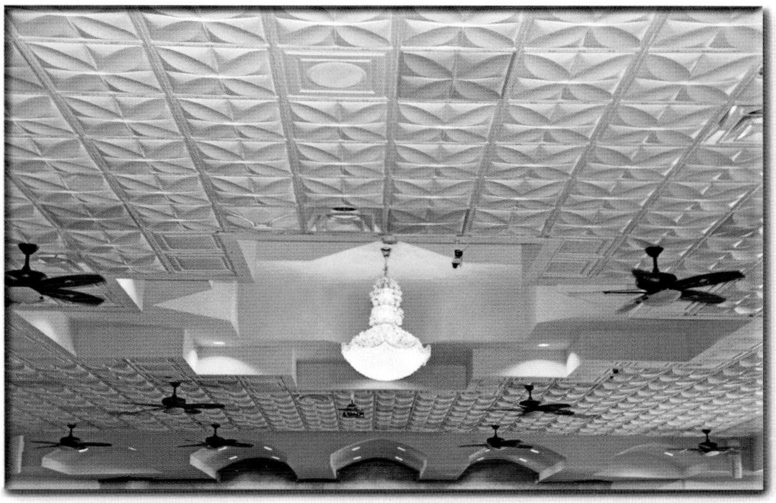

Masjid Maryam (ISGH SWZ) | Sugar Land, TX

Tempe Masjid | Tempe, AZ

Islamic Center of Tucson | Tucson, AZ

Masjid As-Siddiq | Stillwater, OK

Islamic Society of Greater Kansas City | Kansas City, MO

Islamic Center of San Antonio | San Antonio, TX

Islamic Center of Frisco | Frisco, TX

Masjid Al-Emaan | Stockton, CA

Masjid Abu Bakr | Denver, CO

Masjid al-Mustafa | San Jose, CA

Islamic Society of Sarasota & Bradenton
Sarasota, FL

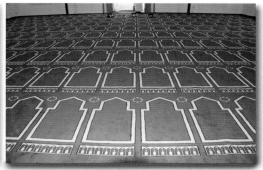

Masjid Nur | Port Charlotte, FL

Noor Musallah | Wesley Chapel, FL

Islamic Center of Fort Collins | Fort Collins, CO

Islamic Center of Northeast Florida | Jacksonville, FL

Masjid Aysha | Lakeland, FL

Dzemat Bosanski Mesdzid | Pinellas Park, FL

281

Iman Mosque | Milwaukee, WI

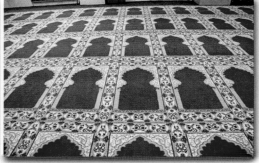

Dar Al-Noor Islamic Center | Manassas, VA

Islamic Center of San Antonio | San Antonio, TX

Quba Islamic Institute | Houston, TX

Masjid El-Farouq | Houston, TX

Masjid Attaqwa (ISGH SWZ) | Sugar Land, TX

Islam In Spanish Centro Islamico | Houston, TX

Masjid Al-Ibrahimi | Ft. Worth, TX

Clear Lake Islamic Center | Clear Lake City, TX

Albanian-American Islamic Center of Queens
Glendale, NY

Masjid Hazrati Abubakr Siddique | Flushing, NY

Dar Al-Dawah Mosque | Astoria, NY

Islamic Center of High Point | High Point, NC

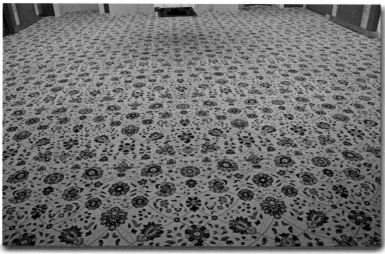

Respect Graduate School | Bethlehem, PA

Islamic Cultural Center of New York | New York, NY

Masjid Bilal Ibn Rabah | St. Louis, MO

Dar Aljalal Mosque | Hazelwood, MO

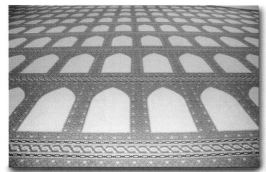

Dar Al-Farooq Center | Minneapolis, MN

Masjid Al-Tawba | Eden Prairie, MN

Masjid At-Tawheed | Grand Rapids, MI

Islamic Center of North Phoenix | Phoenix, AZ

Islamic Center of Shoreline
Shoreline, WA

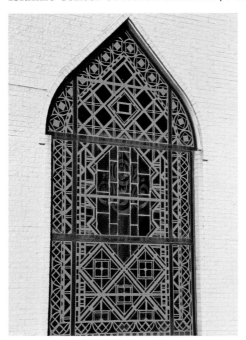

Islamic Center of G.T. | Perrysburg, OH   **Masjid ZamZam** | Dundalk, MD   **Masjid Abubakar Asiddiq** | Columbus, OH

Masjid Darru Salam | Wichita, KS

Masjid-E-Tawheed | Las Vegas, NV

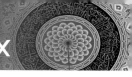

Mission Viejo Masjid | Mission Viejo, CA

Jamia Masjid | Las Vegas, NV

Masjid al-Mustafa | San Jose, CA

Dar al-Islam | Abiquiu, NM

Islamic Com. of Bosniaks
Boise, ID

Noor Islamic Cultural Center | Dublin, OH

Dar Alarkam Mosque | Red Oak, TX

Madina Masjid | Windsor, CT

Parkchester Jame Masjid | Bronx, NY

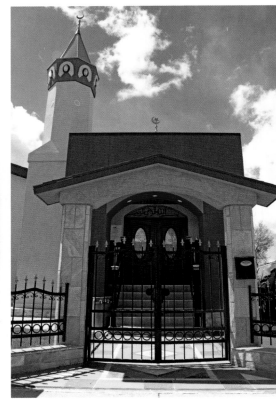

Mosque Maryam | Salt Lake City, UT

Community Mosque of Winston-Salem | Winston-Salem, NC

Masjidul Waritheen | Oakland, CA

Islamic Center of Central Missouri | Columbia, MO

Iranian American Muslim Assoc. of N. America | Los Angeles, CA

Masjid Ar-Rahman | Manteca, CA

Masjid Noor-Ul-Huda | Bronx, NY

Muslim American Society of Philadelphia | Philadelphia, PA

Masjid Darul Quran | Bay Shore, NY

Dar al-Islam | Abiquiu NM

Masjid Annoor
Fort Smith, AR

Islamic Center of Little Rock
Little Rock, AR

Islamic Center of Castroville
Castroville, CA

Masjid Ibrahim
Coachella, CA

Masjid Al-Awwal | Pittsburgh, PA

MAS Youth Center - New York Chapter | Brooklyn, NY

Masjid Alhuda
Buffalo, NY

Masjid Hamza (ISGH SWZ)
Houston, TX

Madina Masjid
New York, NY

Masjid Omar Bin Abdul Aziz
Lilburn, GA

Masjid Musab Bin Omir
Brooklyn, NY

Masjid E Ibrahim
Kingman, AZ

Farmington Valley Am Muslim Ctr
Avon, CT

Masjid Al-Rahman
Orlando, FL

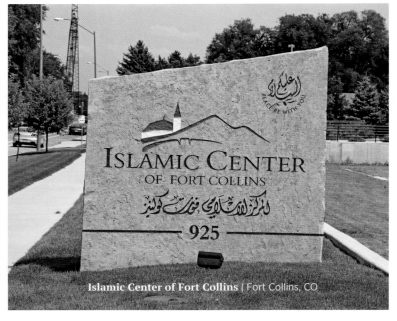

Islamic Center of Fort Collins | Fort Collins, CO

Masjid Al-Jumuah
Bolingbrook, IL

Yusuf Mosque
Brighton, MA

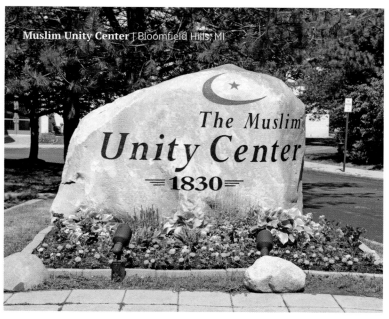

Muslim Unity Center | Bloomfield Hills, MI

The Mosque Cares
Hazel Crest, IL

Masjidul Taqwa
San Diego, CA

Islamic Center of Kansas | Olathe, KS

Masjid Abu Bakr Al-Siddiq | Hayward, CA

Masjid Al-Halim | Sumrall, MS

American Muslim Center
Dearborn, MI

Meca Center of Peoria
Peoria, IL

Islamic Center of Arizona
Phoenix, AZ

Islamic Center of Ewing
Trenton, NJ

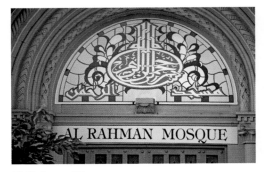

Al-Rahman Mosque
Rochester NY

Masjid Bilal
Cleveland, OH

Masjid An-Nasr
Oklahoma City, OK

Islamic Center of Tri-Cities | West Richland, WA

Islamic Foundation North | Libertyville, IL

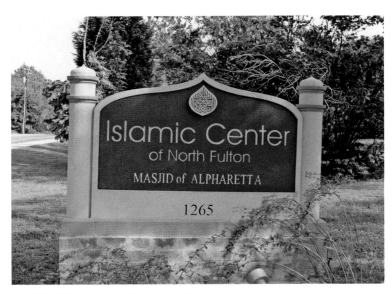

Masjid of Alpharetta | Alpharetta, GA

Islamic Center of Detroit | Detroit, MI

Dalton Islamic Center
Dalton, GA

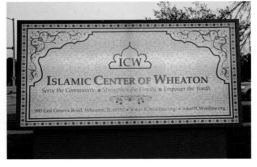

Islamic Center of Wheaton
Wheaton, IL

King Fahad Mosque
Culver City, CA

MAS Islamic Center of Dallas
Richardson, TX

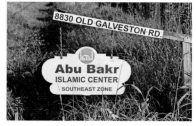

Masjid Abu Bakr Siddique
Houston, TX

Masjid Ar-Rahmah
Redmond, WA

Masjid Dawood
Brooklyn, NY

Muslim American Society of Philadelphia | Philadelphia, PA

Hamzah Islamic Center | Alpharetta, GA

Islamic Center of San Antonio | San Antonio, TX

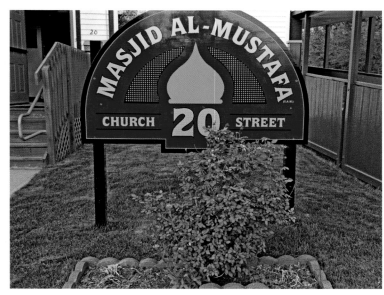

Jamia Masjid Al-Mustafa | East Hartford, CT

Islamic Center of Ocala
Ocala, FL

Masjid Nabawi
Schenectady, NY

Islamic Center of Conejo Valley
Newbury Park, CA

Muslim Community Center
Silver Spring, MD

Islamic Center of Washington | Washington, DC

Ahmad Samawi Mosque | West Chester, OH

King Fahad Mosque | Culver City, CA

Mustafa Center | Annandale, VA

Masjid Abu Bakr Al-Siddiq | Hayward, CA

Islamic Center of Irvine | Irvine, CA

Huntsville Islamic Center | Huntsville, AL,

Islamic Center of Jonesboro | Jonesboro, AR

SABA Islamic Center | San Jose, CA

Islamic Assoc. of Allen | Allen, TX

Khadeeja Masjid | West Valley City, UT

Masjid Al-Israa | Fridley, MN

Islamic Community Center of Illinois | Chicago, IL

Tempe Masjid | Tempe, AZ

Masjid As-Salam (ISGH-North) | Spring, TX

Muslim Community of Western Suburbs
Canton, MI

Masjid Al-Islam | Dallas, TX

Masjid Attakwa | Sioux Falls, SD

Muslims Com. Ctr. of SD | Brookings, SD

Bismarck Muslim Com. Ctr | Bismarck, ND

AlHuda Mosque | Bellbrook, OH

Islamic Center of Rockland | Va

Masjid Abubakar Asiddiq | Columbus, OH

Westchester Muslim Center | Mt. Vernon, NY

Masjid Al-Quran | Dallas, TX

Islamic Center of Maine | Orono, ME

Masjid ISSA | Dover, NH

Masjid Al-Tawheed | Williston, ND

Dar Al-Dawah Mosque | Astoria, NY

Islamic Center of Cheyenne | Cheyenne, WY

je, NY

Islamic Society of Western Massachusetts | West Springfield, MA

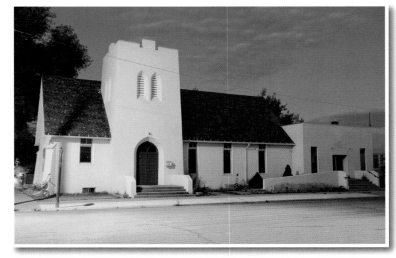

Islamic Center of Laramie | Laramie, WY

Islamic Center In Grand Forks | Grand Forks, ND

The Islamic Center of Athens | Athens, OH

Islamic Soc. of Wichita Falls | Wichita Falls, TX

Masjid Al-Farooq | Prestonsburg, KY

Khursheed Unissa Memorial Community Center | Amarillo, TX

ICNE Sharon Masjid | Sharon, MA

Masjid Omar Ibn Sayyid | Fayetteville, NC

MAS Islamic Center of Dallas | Richardson, TX

Masjid Abu Bakr | Anchorage, AK

Islamic Association of Raleigh | Raleigh, NC

Association of Bosniaks of New Hampshire | Hooksett, NH

Islamic Association of Allen | Allen, TX

Islamic Society of Vermont | Colchester, VT

Islamic Center of Siouxland | South Sioux City, NE

Institute of Islamic Learning in Metroplex | Plano, TX

Butte Islamic Center | Butte, MT

Islamic Center of Naperville | Naperville, IL

Islamic Society of Greater Augusta | Augusta, ME

al-Masjid al-Awwal | Pittsburgh, PA

Islamic Association of West Virginia | Charleston, WV

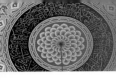

Grand Strand Islamic Center | Myrtle Beach, SC

Magnolia Islamic Center | Madison, MS

Masjid Al-Muslimiin | Columbia, SC

Masjid Al-Hidayah | Gulfport, MS

Masjid Wali Aziz | Vicksburg, MS

Conway Islamic Center | Conway, SC

Central Mosque of Charleston | Charleston, SC

Masjid Omar | Moscow, ID

Masjid Al-Aman | Middletown, NJ

Masjid as-Sunnah | Anchorage, AK